Happy 30th Anniversary
to
Mike & Sher ~

from

Mom

D1590070

Dearly Beloved

By David Wilkerson

Dearly Beloved

David Wilkerson

ISBN 0-9712187-4-9

Printed in the United States of America

Copyright © 2009 by David Wilkerson Publications, Inc.

Contents

Introduction

It has been my privilege to share my messages preached at Times Square Church with a great host of readers throughout the United States and around the world. Along with each message, I included a short one-page letter of encouragement. Over the past twenty years these "cover letters" became a source of much blessing and encouragement to our readers. Every letter began with this greeting: "Dearly Beloved."

Numbers of readers wrote to us requesting these letters be published as a daily devotional book. We prayed much about it and received confirmation to proceed with the project. *Dearly Beloved* is a compilation of letters selected as being the most effective, as measured by the many testimonies we have received from our readers.

I trust these letters will prove to be spiritual meat to every hungry reader. They are presented here as daily readings. I do not recommend reading more than one or two selections a day. The reader needs time to prayerfully digest a little at a time, and should ask the Holy Spirit to illuminate it and apply it to the heart and mind.

Also included in this book are several of my preached messages from Times Square Church which have appeared as newsletters. Like the "Dearly Beloved" letters, these are meant to provide spiritual nourishment to readers.

Keep this book close at hand, especially for difficult and trying times. Included in these letters and preached messages are words for times of crisis. You can go back and read certain chapters over again, each time gaining new strength and spiritual encouragement.

May the Holy Spirit open your eyes and deliver to you God's Word in season.

DAVID WILKERSON
Times Square Church
New York City

Part 1
Dearly Beloved Letters

Dearly Beloved: **1**

MAY THE LOVE OF GOD SHINE UPON YOU.

These words of Jesus touch my soul: *"Be not therefore anxious, saying, what shall we eat? Or what shall we drink? Or how shall we be clothed? For after all these things do the Gentiles seek"* (Matthew 6:31-32).

Jesus is warning about the heathen tendency to worry. He tells us that worry — over our job, our family, our future, our survival — is a heathen's way of living. It is the attitude of those who have no heavenly Father. They do not know God as he desires to be known: as a caring, providing, loving Father in heaven.

To all who believe, it is not enough to know God only as the Almighty, the Creator, the Lord of all. He also wants us to know him as our heavenly Father. *"For your heavenly Father knoweth that you have need of all these things"* (6:32).

"Take therefore no thought for tomorrow" (6:34). With these plain words, Jesus commands us: "Do not give a thought, a single worry, to what might or might not happen tomorrow. You can't change anything. And you can't help anything by worrying. When you do, you're only doing as the heathen do."

Jesus then says, *"Seek ye first the kingdom of God and his righteousness; and all these things shall be added unto you"* (6:33). In other words, we are to go on loving Jesus. We are to move on, casting all our cares on him. And we are to rest in his faithfulness. Our heavenly Father will see to it that we are supplied with all the essential things of life.

I wonder if the angels are baffled by all the worry and anxiousness of those who claim to trust in the Lord. To those celestial beings, it must seem insulting to God that we worry as if we had no caring Father in heaven. What perplexing questions the angels must ask among themselves:

"Do they not believe the One who loves them? Did he not tell them he knows about all their needs? Do they not know the Father sends us to take charge of them in times of danger? Do they not believe that he who feeds the birds, the fish, the whole animal kingdom will feed and clothe them? How can they fret and worry when they know God possesses all power, all wealth, and can supply the needs of all creation? How can they accuse him of neglect, as if he isn't true to his Word?"

The birds sing, while we complain and speak of fear and anxiety. The lilies of the field stand tall in their glory, while we wilt and bend before the smallest wind of adversity.

The following poem puts it succinctly:

The very birds reprove thee with all their happy song;
    the very flowers teach thee that fretting is a wrong.
"Cheer up," the sparrow chirpeth. "Thy Father feedeth me;
    think how much he careth, oh lovely child, for thee."
"Fear not," the flowers whisper; "since thus he hath arrayed
    the buttercup and daisy. How canst thou be afraid?"

Then don't you trouble trouble, till trouble troubles you.
You'll only double trouble, and trouble others too.

You most definitely have a heavenly Father. Trust in him!

Dearly Beloved: 2

MAY THE LORD JESUS BLESS AND KEEP YOU IN ALL YOUR WAYS.

We hear so many reports today of depravity, terror, hatred and political turmoil, it seems to overload our senses. There is so much bad news, so much division and distortion on all sides.

In the midst of all this restlessness and disorder, I hear God's Word telling me to rejoice greatly and be glad. It says, *"Let the saints be joyful in glory: let them sing aloud upon their beds"* (Psalm 149:5). When was the last time you sang joyfully, out loud in your bed, before retiring? *"Let Israel rejoice in him that made him: let the children of Zion be joyful in their King"* (149:2). This is faith, when you can sing and rejoice in a time of great turmoil.

If we listen to the so-called experts in the media, we may open ourselves to a spirit of unrest and anger. We can get caught up in issues that are not eternal but are soon to pass. I refuse to be caught up in the present political rage. I will go to the voting booth and cast my ballot, yet not according to my feelings but on the basis of biblical truth. I will vote calmly, without losing my peace or my love for lost humanity.

Most of all, I will obey God's eternal Word and rejoice and be glad, no matter how fiercely the storms rage around me. We are told to sing and rejoice — and we must do so, knowing our God has promised to lead and protect us through it all. Consider David's testimony:

"Thou art my hiding place; thou shalt preserve me from trouble; thou shalt compass me about with songs of deliverance" (Psalm 32:7). *"Be glad in the Lord, and rejoice, ye righteous: and shout for joy, all ye that are upright in heart"* (32:11).

God sits as King over the flood. He has everything under control, and there is no need to fear or despair. Our Lord is in our midst, and one day all his enemies will become his footstool. Thus, we are told, *"Shout unto God with a voice of triumph...for he is King over all the earth"* (47:1-2).

In a time when Christ says men's hearts will *"fail them with fear"* over what they see happening in the world, his people are to *"look up, and lift up your heads; for your redemption draweth nigh"* (Luke 21:28).

Can you do this? Will you do it? Will you sing at night, and be glad and rejoice through the day? Look up, lift your head, and be glad with hope.

Dearly Beloved: 3

JESUS IS LORD NOW AND FOREVER.

Some months after 9/11, a New York City newspaper ran this headline: "CITY OF JITTERS." Homeland Security had warned that a planned terrorist strike had been uncovered, and the terror alert had been raised to code orange.

That same day, a New York City police officer spoke to me about the uncertainty and alarm within the police force and fire departments. Their macho exteriors hid secret fears because most of them had lost friends during the 9/11 attacks.

Even now, years later, each time some New Yorkers travel through tunnels and over bridges they hold their breath and pray for protection. A stalled vehicle can cause panic. Subway riders board trains with great apprehension. The greatest fear that haunts this city is a suitcase bomb, carrying nuclear or germ capabilities. Many people began carrying small gas masks. The citizenry seem to be resigned to the inevitable, believing an attack of major proportions will eventually strike. No one knows when, but the thought hangs heavily over the populace.

Yet there is no fear among true believers. Instead, we want to be available should an attack come, to help in the time of crisis. This is how our church has prepared our people. In the midst of these apprehensive times, the Spirit of God is moving in a marvelous way. Many are coming to Christ throughout New York City, and there is an increasing hunger for God among young people especially.

May this be the heart attitude of all of God's servants in these days of apprehension and fear. The Lord has removed all fear from his people, that they may be a source of help to the world in a time of trouble.

Dearly Beloved: **4**

JESUS CHRIST IS LORD NOW AND FOREVER. GLORY TO HIS PRECIOUS NAME!

So much distress. So much affliction. So much sorrow caused by sickness, disease and disaster. So many hurting believers. So many people facing financial crises. The Bible does tell us, *"Many are the afflictions of the righteous…"* However, the second part of this verse changes the meaning entirely: *"…but the Lord delivereth him out of them all"* (Psalm 34:19).

David cried, *"Lord, remember David, and all his afflictions"* (132:1). This godly man faced many troubles. His prayer was,

"Lord, you have delivered others out of their afflictions. Don't forget about me. Help me, deliver me."

The apostle Paul also endured many afflictions. He wrote, *"The Holy Ghost witnesseth [tells me] in every city, saying that bonds and afflictions abide me [await me]" (Acts 20:23)*. Paul added, *"No man should be moved by these afflictions" (1 Thessalonians 3:3)*. He was saying, "Dear saints, don't question why I have to face so many great afflictions. These things do not cause me to question God."

"But in all things approving ourselves as the ministers of God, in much patience, in afflictions, in necessities, in distresses" (2 Corinthians 6:4). Note Paul's emphasis here: "in much patience." Have you been losing patience in your affliction? Have you become so discouraged you've come to the point of casting aside your faith?

A pastor and his wife wrote to me, "We are so discouraged. We have been so mistreated and unappreciated. We are financially devastated and we see very little fruit from our labors. We have prayed, believed and held onto faith. But now we are at the end of endurance. We do not want to doubt, but we need a miracle. We need to see at least some token for good so we can go on."

Any words I have to encourage the downcast seem inadequate. But this one thing I do know: we serve a kind and loving heavenly Father. His Word says he is touched with the feelings of our afflictions. And it is my firm belief that even now he waits for you to lay down all your fears, anxieties, questions — all your cares and burdens — and trust he will deliver you because of his lovingkindness for you.

Lay hold of the following Scriptures and let faith arise in your heart. God has not forgotten you.

- Psalm 117:2: *"For his merciful kindness is great toward us: and the truth of the Lord endureth forever. Praise ye the Lord."*

- Psalm 119:76: *"Let, I pray thee, thy merciful kindness be for my comfort, according to thy word unto thy servant."*

- Isaiah 54:7-8, 10: *"For a small moment have I forsaken thee; but with great mercies will I gather thee. In a little wrath I hid my face from thee for a moment; but with everlasting kindness will I have mercy on thee, saith the Lord thy Redeemer. For the mountains shall depart, and the hills be removed; but my kindness shall not depart from thee, neither shall the covenant of my peace be removed, saith the Lord that hath mercy on thee."*

Dearly Beloved: 5

GREETINGS IN THE PRECIOUS NAME OF OUR LORD JESUS.

The following word was given to me by the Holy Spirit. It is for those who need an answer to prayer, who need help in a time of trouble, and who are ready and willing to move God's heart according to his Word:

1. Lay hold of the covenant promise in Psalm 46:1: *"God is our refuge and strength, a very present help in trouble."* The phrase "very present" means "always available, immediately accessible." Faith must rest in the assurance that God's Spirit abides in you all hours of the day and night, continually. And because he took up a habitation in you, he listens to your every prayerful thought and cry. We know that if he hears us he will grant our petitions. Indeed, the Holy Spirit will move heaven and earth for any child of God who takes time to pour out his heart to the Father with unrushed, unhurried time in his presence.

2. Read and believe Psalm 62:5-7. This is the prayer of David that touched God's heart. David said, in essence, "Wait on God only. Expect help from no other source. He alone must be your provision, your only hope and defense. Only he can supply you with the strength to keep going until your answer comes."

When you become wholly dependent on the Lord alone — when you stop looking to man for help, and trust God for the supernatural — nothing will be able to shake you. Nothing can move you into fits of despair. David declared, *"I shall not be moved"* (Psalm 62:6).

3. Here is the heart of it all, the secret to prevailing prayer that every saint throughout history has learned: THE POURING OUT OF THE HEART BEFORE THE LORD. *"Trust in him at all times; ye people, pour out your heart before him: God is a refuge for us"* (Psalm 62:8). Hannah is our example. Desperate for a child, she "poured out" her soul to the Lord. And, Scripture says, *"Her countenance was no more sad"* (1 Samuel 1:18).

God will hear and answer you when he sees you're willing to shut off all worldly voices for a season. Cry out the contents of your heart, pour out your soul before him, and trust he will respond. The time has come for brokenness before the Lord, for a faith born out of contrite intercession. Follow these scriptural ways, and God will hear and answer.

Dearly Beloved: 6

GOD IS FAITHFUL, WHO HAS PROMISED.

I am deeply blessed by God's message to his people in Psalm

37. I simply have to recommend that you read this Psalm before the day is over. It is one of the richest, most encouraging passages in God's Word. No matter what you may be going through, no matter how trying your situation, this Psalm will be a source of great strength and encouragement to you.

Psalm 37:7 is of special interest to me in light of what is happening in the gay community. States are passing laws that pave the way for gay marriages and hundreds of homosexuals have gotten married. I was so deeply grieved at this lawlessness and mockery of true, God-ordained marriage, I cried, "Oh, Lord, they are stealing our nation. They are mocking your holy Word. America is now indulging in a sin not even known in Sodom and Gomorrah. There is no biblical record of gays marrying in those wicked societies."

Then I read Psalm 37:7: *"Fret not thyself because of him who prospereth in his way, because of the man who bringeth wicked devices to pass."* In other words: "Do not let it get at your spirit. Do not get worked up about it. God hears the deep inner groanings of his people, and he is very patient."

Even so, a line is now being crossed. And God says when that happens, *"Evildoers shall be cut off...the Lord shall laugh at him...and their plots...for he seeth that his day is coming"* (Psalm 37:9, 13).

Let no evildoer think for a moment that God is going to over-look blatant disobedience and mockery of his Word. All through the Bible, we see the Lord sending judgment when lawlessness envelops a society. Let the scoffers laugh, but soon the world will witness God's answer to these satanic attacks against his plan for marriage. Christ likened the female, the wife, to the church, which he calls his bride. Now Satan has caused ridicule of this biblical type and moved many Americans to reject the Bible as the final moral rule of law.

Soon God is going to breathe his wrath on every Sodom-like community with judgments unlike any this generation has seen. Everyone will know that God has a controversy with this nation. I believe he has already cried, "Enough! The hour of chastisement has come."

Pray for our nation amid these times. God hears the prayers of his people.

Dearly Beloved: 7

GOD IS GREAT AND GREATLY TO BE PRAISED!

In Acts 3:19, Peter speaks of "times of refreshing" that would come from being in the Lord's presence. I am convinced that even now, amid times of global turmoil, the church is experiencing such a time of refreshing. It is an event in which Jesus is manifesting his presence worldwide.

Yes, there is much spiritual deadness and dryness in many churches. Multitudes of believers have compromised their walk with Jesus, while others have gone mad after worldly pleasures. Many preachers have diluted the gospel and become more like entertainers than ministers of God's pure and holy Word.

But something glorious is happening all over the world, even in Islamic nations. There is undeniable evidence that the Holy Spirit is hovering over nations, and the awesome presence of Christ is manifesting powerfully. It is happening throughout Russia, China, South America, Africa, Asia and nearly every nation on earth. God is stirring people in Mongolia and in the former Soviet states. In India the Spirit of God is mightily at work, as well as in nations that have never had a Christian presence.

I hear of such times of refreshing touching various towns and cities in the United States. Pastors are growing desperate for a true manifestation of God's presence in their churches. They do not want hype or watered-down, sinner-appealing messages. They are tired of programs with expensive, market-driven tapes, books and manmade concepts. Their cry is now, "We want the Holy Spirit. We want to bring Jesus' presence back. More than crowds, we want Christ manifested."

This refreshing of Christ's manifest presence is the result of exaltation of him alone — not signs and wonders, not spiritual gifts, not "revival" that soon fades. This is a last-days revelation of the glory and power of Christ. Many write to me saying they go to church yearning to experience the actual presence of Jesus. They want to hear from a shepherd who has been shut in with the Lord. They don't want any more entertainment, showmanship or empty methods. Now they're crying, "Give me Christ. Give me the melting, healing, awesome presence of Jesus."

May this be the heart-cry of all God's people in these days.

Dearly Beloved: 8

THE LORD BE PRAISED!

During prayer the Holy Spirit led me to Psalm 56. This word is meant for those who have been wounded — whether by family, friends, or the words and actions of the ungodly.

It is a word also for those who love the Lord yet who shed tears and carry burdens that seem to grow heavier by the day. Some believers wake up every day under a cloud of fear and despair. Financial problems can crush and frighten. Others face serious health battles and insufferable pain. Some grieve over family members who are in deep trouble, perhaps in rebellion against the Lord.

Hear the blessed Word of God directed to you in your hour of need:

• Psalm 56:3: *"When I am afraid, I will put my trust in Thee. [I shall not be afraid.]"*

• Psalm 56:4: *"I will praise his Word. In God I have put my trust; I will not fear what man can do to me."*

• Psalm 56:8: *"Thou tellest [take notice of] my wanderings [sorrow, feelings of loss]: put thou my tears into thy bottle: are they not in thy book?"*

• Psalm 56:9: *"When I cry unto thee, then shall my enemies turn back: this I know; for God is for me."*

• Psalm 56:13: *"For thou hast delivered my soul from death: will you not deliver my feet from falling, that I might walk before God in the light of the living?"*

These are anointed words from the Spirit of God. I encourage you to pray over each verse listed and lay claim to it by faith. The Lord knows all about your struggles and pain. He knows every detail of your situation, and he hears even the unspoken cries of your broken heart.

All that the Lord asks of us is unwavering faith. According to James 1:3, God does test our faith, but *"the trying of your faith worketh patience."* If we need wisdom, we are instructed to ask in faith: *"If any of you lack wisdom, let him ask of God, that giveth to all men liberally, and upbraideth not; and it shall be given him. But let him ask in faith, nothing wavering. For he that wavereth is like a wave of the sea driven with the wind and tossed. For let not that man think that he shall receive any thing of the Lord"* (James 1:5-7).

Heed the words we have been given: *"What time I am afraid, I will trust in thee."* I have always preached, "The hardest part of faith is the last half hour," just before the answer comes. Your cries and prayers have been heard by the Lord. Even now he is doing his secret, behind-the-scenes work of deliverance. Until then, he will give you mercy and strength to bear it.

Dearly Beloved: 9

MAY THE LOVE OF JESUS SHINE ON YOU.

As we read Paul's epistles, we often find him sharing very personal matters with his readers. Please bear with me as I share a few personal things with you.

A few years ago, my wife, Gwen, had knee replacement surgery, her twenty-first operation (five for cancer). She told me this was the most painful operation of all.

The Lord has seen our family through deep waters of affliction over the years. Both of our daughters, Debi and Bonnie, also are cancer survivors. God has graciously delivered Gwen from a cloud of guilt she carried for a long time, thinking she had "passed on cancer" to them. Doctors called it a cancer cluster. Today, Gwen, Debi and Bonnie are all doing well — God be praised.

In 2003, our young granddaughter, Tiffany, died of brain cancer. This was especially difficult for Gwen, who had to fight off the same old accusations from Satan that Tiffany's cancer was also hereditary. The Holy Spirit has been so faithful to comfort and heal the hurt. We know God always does what is best for all concerned.

As I look back over fifty years of ministry, I recall innumerable tests, trials and times of crushing pain. But through it all the Lord has proven faithful, loving and totally true to all his promises. Our ministry is debt free, and we have not had to beg or plead for finances. We have faced huge burdens, both personal and ministry related, but we have come through them all with joy unspeakable.

May you draw on your history of God's faithfulness to you, in the midst of your trial.

Dearly Beloved: 10

TO CHRIST BE ALL GLORY, HONOR AND PRAISE.

May I give you a word I believe is from the mind of Christ through the Holy Spirit? It has to do with what I believe is one of the greatest needs in the church today. Indeed, it is a word every believer ought to hear.

This is the word: Growing numbers of Christians are no longer fully satisfied with Christ. The Lord is being dethroned by what he himself called thorns. Jesus defined thorns as the cares of this world, the deceitfulness of riches, the lusts of other things entering into the heart. Christ said these are the thorns that choke the Word and cause it to become unfruitful.

I ask you, is the Lord more on your mind than a year ago? Do you spend more time in his presence than a year ago? Is your passion for him growing or withering?

Many of those who once were passionately in love with Christ now run about pursuing their own interests. They're burdened down with stress and problems, chasing after riches and the things of this world. They have grown cold or lukewarm, and they have less and less time for Jesus. The Lord and his church now get only an hour of their time, on Sunday mornings.

Jesus said, *"If a man abide not in me, he is cast forth as a branch, and is withered"* (John 15:6). In other words, that person is drying up, no longer drawing life from the true vine. He is deceived by thinking all is well, because he still speaks the language of the intimacy he once enjoyed with Christ.

Of course, riches and the things that are necessary in life are not evil in themselves. All of us face cares and troubles in this life. The sin comes in the effort, time and energy we spend in pursuing these things, at the expense of neglecting Christ.

One day soon we all will stand before our blessed Christ to face his judgment seat. We will see him face to face. I want to stand in my Lord's presence as a fruitful son, not ushered into his presence as a lukewarm, withered, estranged, thorn-choked servant.

I hear the Holy Spirit calling the Lord's people back to their first love. Back to hungering and thirsting for more of Christ. Back to spending quality time in his presence. Back to loving his Word. Back to casting all cares upon him. Back to depending on him for guidance.

Christ desires intimacy with his bride. He yearns after his beloved to return to him with love and obedience. I humbly submit this word to you, trusting the Holy Spirit will stir your heart and draw you closer to himself.

Dearly Beloved: 11

GOD BE PRAISED FOR HIS MERCY AND GOODNESS.
I have no ghost writers. I personally write every message and

every piece of published mail. And I have written the message you are now reading. I go to the Lord and ask him to show me what to say. I ask the Holy Spirit to help me send a word of hope and blessing from the Scriptures.

The Holy Spirit has directed me to go to Psalm 32. God says there, *"I will instruct thee and teach thee in the way which thou shalt go: I will guide thee with mine eye" (Psalm 32:8)*. I believe the Lord instructed me to share the following message with you. It may not apply to everyone, but many will know that the Lord has spoken personally to their present need. THIS IS WHAT I HEAR FROM THE HOLY SPIRIT:

Jesus said to his disciples, "The fields are white, ready to harvest." The harvest is an ingathering of souls in the last days. And the law of the harvest is this: the darker the days, the whiter the harvest. Right now, many souls are ripe for harvest all over the world. We see this everywhere we go in ministry.

But there is another harvest in these last days also. The Lord was speaking prophetically about what he foresaw coming in our time: a harvest of golden-ripe faith in the hearts of his people. Our Lord wants a tested, suffering people who will rise up in the midst of distress and trouble and proclaim, "I trust my God!"

Jesus does not expect faith from the worldly crowd. When he wondered aloud, "Will I find faith on the earth when I return?" he was not speaking of sinners. But we who love him are also told, *"He that trusteth in the Lord, mercy shall compass him about" (Psalm 32:10)*. God promises that his goodness is *"laid up...for them that trust in thee before the sons of men" (31:19)*.

I can say with the Psalmist David, "I have known trouble, much suffering, financial need, the sorrow of the deaths of loved ones, the slander of those I loved who turned against me. I have known personal pain. There were times I thought things were hopeless. Times of temptation. Times of weeping until there were no tears left."

Some of my suffering was self-imposed, caused by ignorance or foolishness. But now, at seventy-seven years of age, I can boldly testify: God has never failed me. Through all the trouble, pain and sufferings, I have come through with joy and a strong trust in the goodness and faithfulness of the Lord. Here is the testimony he desires to hear from all of his tested children: *"Be glad in the Lord, and rejoice...and shout for joy, all ye that are upright in heart"* (32:11).

We rejoice in the faithfulness of our Lord.

Dearly Beloved: 12

GRACE, PEACE AND MERCY TO YOU IN CHRIST.

A scientist said of the catastrophe, "The whole world shook." Another called it "the worst natural disaster in the world's history." They were describing the underwater earthquake that devastated entire coasts in Asia a few years ago. An island in the Indian Ocean moved nearly 100 feet. Tens of thousands were left dead.

When awful disasters of this magnitude strike, I always go to the Father asking, "Lord, what is this all about? Is there something you're trying to tell humankind? Was this simply an unexplainable accident of nature, or is there something your people ought to know as to why it happened?"

We all sorrow and mourn for the indescribable pain and misery endured by multitudes. We have prayed earnestly for those afflicted. Our ministry has sent thousands of dollars through Christian relief agencies to help rebuild churches and homes in devastated areas. Scripture tells us our heavenly Father is touched by the very feelings of the wounded. The Holy Spirit pours out comfort to all believers in the nations affected.

America is a giving nation and very compassionate. I thank God for the response of so many who prayed, gave and went to those areas to help. But something deep within my soul troubled me. The magnitude of the disaster didn't sink in. We seem to be numbed, stupefied by it all.

I thank God for good reports of blessings in areas of the world, including America. But if we cannot be brought to our knees by such unleashed power — if we cannot humble ourselves after witnessing the worst natural disaster in world history, the entire globe trembling — what will it take to silence the God-mockers? Are we now shockproof?

Think of the expulsion of God from our society in the name of political correctness...the whole world turning to secularism and materialism...a church growing more worldly than the world itself...the rise of violence and apathy, more so than in Noah's day...the Bible no longer being accepted as God's Word...a day "when everything that can be shaken is being shaken"...when power is unleashed that is one million times more powerful than the atomic bomb dropped on Hiroshima...when thoughtful people everywhere have an intuition that "somebody is tinkering with nature, something is happening that cannot be explained away"...when society continues its business without a single "God pause," without even a thought that God will not be mocked. THAT IS THE TIME WHEN WE HAVE COME NEAR OR CROSSED A LINE INTO A SPIRITUAL STUPOR THAT NO AMOUNT OF DIVINE MERCY CAN AWAKEN.

God is merciful, gracious and ready to forgive. Jesus died to save this lost world; he did not come to destroy, maim or pour out wrath. Out of the terror and pain of the passion of Christ, redemption came. May Jesus demonstrate his love and compassion through his disciples as the day of the Lord approaches.

Dearly Beloved: **13**

SPECIAL GREETINGS IN CHRIST.

Here is a word from the Lord for you: *"BE OF GOOD COUR-AGE, AND HE SHALL STRENGTHEN YOUR HEART, ALL YE THAT HOPE IN THE LORD" (Psalm 31:24)*.

Sometime soon we are going to see America falling under more token judgments. These calamities will come as warnings of the all-powerful judgment that throughout history has fallen upon every nation that forsakes the Lord.

God has stirred my heart once again to speak forth prophetic warnings about what he is about to do. I am of the opinion that righteous, praying Christians will know what the Lord is doing and will not be taken by surprise. The ungodly won't receive Holy Ghost warnings delivered by God's true watchmen — but those who love Jesus ought to be thankful for such prophetic light, no matter how gloomy it may seem. The Lord has never in history judged a nation without first clearly warning the people of his intentions. *"Surely the Lord will do nothing, but he revealeth his secret unto his servants the prophets" (Amos 3:7)*.

Many believers have made it clear they don't want to hear any "doomsday" preaching. But I must obey the Lord and preach the messages he gives me. I believe most Christians want to hear what God is saying about the future, and he uses certain servants to deliver that word.

For your encouragement, would you take time to "spiritually devour" the following Scriptures from the Psalms? I urge you to mark them in your Bible as a powerful source of encouragement throughout the year:

• Psalm 32:7-8 • 31:19-24 • 32:7-8 • 34:4, 6-10 • 34: 7-19 • 46:1-11 • 69:13-18.

These verses can strengthen your faith every single day of the year. They are some of the most powerful words of encouragement in all of God's Word. May the Lord bless your reading of them in these troubled times.

Dearly Beloved: 14

MAY THE LORD BLESS YOU MIGHTILY.

When you pray, you can expect to enrage hell. Satan will come against you, against Christ's church, and he will try to bring ruin, reproach and turmoil.

The church cannot be ready for revival if we are afraid of the darkness and intimidation of the devil and his forces. Satan has tried to intimidate us here in New York City. At one time, Satanists etched demonic emblems on the glass doors of the entrance to our church. Police experts told us the signs signified death and human sacrifice. When our people saw the symbols they prayed all the more diligently. No one was intimidated.

We are never to fear the devil, never to tremble at his schemes and plots against us. We serve a tender, loving heavenly Father who will never abandon us into the hand of our enemy. So rejoice, take heart and trust your caring Father.

You will come out of your battle in peace, because God never abandons a single child of his.

Dearly Beloved: **15**

GREETINGS IN THE PRECIOUS NAME OF THE LORD.

When I sit down to write a personal note to our readers, I pray, "Lord, give me something for your people that will edify and encourage all who are cast down, all who are going through a time of testing."

As I prayed those words for this message, the Lord directed me to three different passages of Scripture. Each is for a different kind of situation that some may be facing. God is faithful to his children, and he sends his Word to them in perfect time. My prayer is that you will be given a direct word of encouragement from at least one of the following portions of Scripture:

1. If you are being tested by those who have risen up against you — if you are being slandered or gossiped about — READ ALL OF PSALM 109.

2. If you are downcast, distressed, wondering if your trial of faith will ever end — READ ALL OF PSALM 18.

3. If you are wondering why God has not yet answered your desperate prayer or supplied your need — READ THE FOLLOWING PORTIONS FROM THE PSALMS:

• Psalm 21:1-2 • Psalm 22:24 • Psalm 31:7-8 • Psalm 31:19-24 • Psalm 32:7-8 • Psalm 33:18-19

May the Lord send His Word and heal you.

Dearly Beloved: **16**

BLESSINGS TO YOU IN THE NAME OF THE LORD.

I have a very special word from the Lord, for a particular few who are right now going through a great trial. As I sat down to write this message, the Holy Spirit prompted me to set aside everything I was going to say and speak to just a few, with a personal word of hope from the Lord.

Thousands will read this same word — but what I am writing is directed to a select few who will know immediately who they are. This word is directed to those who this very moment are at a point of despair, unable to shake off a feeling of abandonment. You are in a situation that has drained all your strength, leaving you to wonder if God has turned a deaf ear to your crying. You have even questioned the power or effectiveness of prayer, because you haven't seen any evidence of an answer. You don't want to accuse God of neglecting you; you want to show him a measure of faith. But you are confused — BECAUSE NOTHING CHANGES.

THIS WORD IS FOR YOU — STRAIGHT FROM THE HEART OF YOUR CARING, LOVING HEAVENLY FATHER:

1. God's eye is still on you. You have not been forsaken.

- *"Behold, the eye of the Lord is upon them that fear him, upon them that hope in his mercy"* (Psalm 33:18).

- *"The eyes of the Lord are upon the righteous, and his ears are open unto their cry"* (34:15).

2. Keep crying out to him. God is teaching you to depend on him wholly in spite of your circumstances.

- *"I sought the Lord, and he heard me, and delivered me from all my fears"* (34:4).

- *"The righteous cry, and the Lord heareth, and delivereth them out of all their troubles"* (34:17).

- *"Many are the afflictions of the righteous: but the Lord delivereth him out of them all"* (34:19).

3. Finally, go to Psalm 56 — and prepare your heart to hear directly from the throne of God. Read the whole chapter. IT IS FOR YOU — TODAY — AS IF THE LORD HIMSELF HAS COME PERSONALLY TO YOUR HOUSE TO SPEAK ONLY TO YOU.

What a wonderful Lord, who knows just what we need — and whose Word and deliverance are always on time.

Dearly Beloved: **17**

MAY THE LORD CAUSE HIS FACE TO SHINE ON YOU.

I want to talk to you about "soul sickness." This is caused by a flood of troubles coming upon you — not just one problem, but one after another. King David cried, *"Save me, O God, for waters are come in unto my soul. I sink in deep mire. I am come into deep waters, floods overflowing. I am weary of my crying"* (Psalm 69:1-3).

Troubles came at David so powerfully he thought he would collapse. He prayed, *"Be gracious to me, O Lord, for I am so distressed. I am wasting away from grief. My strength faileth, my soul and my belly"* (31:9).

Some readers may say, "I have known troubles, but not a flood of them. I can't relate to David's pain. I can't relate to Job's afflictions." But I am speaking to those who are facing a flood of fears: fear of losing a job. Fear about finances. Fear about marriage or children. Fear about world conditions. Right now, multitudes of elderly people are living on starvation means. Parents grieve over children who are drawn away by drug and alcohol-addicted friends. Couples have mounting mortgage payments, troubled marriages, bills piling up.

I have been called a doomsday preacher. Some have even asked to be taken off my mailing list because they say I am too negative. But I can't help speaking about what I see and hear. Chat with your neighbors — listen as they express their heartsickness over the hell breaking out in schools, the politically correct messes foisted on kids, teaching that is so immoral and godless it sickens the soul.

The root cause of soul sickness is when your troubles go on…when events get worse…when your soul cries out to God for help…and there seems to be no answer. Soul sickness is to know the Lord, to love him, to pray and even to shed tears, and still he does not seem to be there.

David said his troubles became so overwhelming, his soul was cast down "so that I cannot even speak." In other words: "I have cried so much, there are no tears left. All I can see now is despair in the days ahead."

If you relate to this at all, I have hopeful news for you. Here are simple, uncomplicated, biblical truths that can heal your soul sickness:

• Most important of all, keep praying, even when the situation worsens. God is going to answer in his time, in ways you could not imagine. The hardest part of faith is the last half hour, just before the answer comes.

• Even as important: do not get mad at God — ever! I see this happening to believers worldwide. All unbelief and impatience imply that the Lord has picked you out of the masses in the world and made you the object of cruelty and harassment. God forbid! He loves you through all your struggles. If he were to shut his ear to your cries, he would be a fraud — and he is not. He is your loving, forgiving, almighty, caring Father.

Shake off fear, because it has torment. Instead, rest in his promises. Things may change — your lifestyle may have to be simplified because of circumstances — but all things do work together for good to them that love God and are called according to his purpose.

Look up — God will never fail you!

Dearly Beloved: 18

MAY GOD BLESS YOU WITH MUCH PEACE AND JOY.

I would like to use this message to speak about anger. As I was meditating, I came across a letter on my desk from a Christian woman who wrote:

"I prayed about a certain situation in my life and my prayer was not answered. In fact, the very opposite happened. Because of this, I allowed unbelief to develop in my heart. My unbelief caused me to be angry with God. It frightened me to think that, as a human being, I would be angry with the living God. Since then, I have repented — and not only has my situation been changed, but my faith has been restored. I still trust God completely with my situation."

Over the years, I have seen that when people harbor anger against someone, bitterness follows. If they are not delivered, they end up hating God, even though they wouldn't admit it. The truth is, often the Lord does not answer us according to our petitions, but in a way that tests his faithfulness in our eyes. You may think your prayer has been denied — but what you see happening instead may be part of his perfect plan, even though you think it is a disaster. God has a way of accomplishing a fuller, more blessed outcome by turning apparent disaster into a glorious miracle.

Anger, resentment, unforgiveness — all are of Satan and result in hardness of heart. These are root sins that ruin many lives worldwide. I do not know who I am writing to on this subject; in fact, you may be free of all anger. But we must take heed, lest a little root of anger is left to sprout and grow into a life-controlling addiction.

I know God is speaking to someone reading this. And he is saying, in essence: "LAY DOWN THAT ANGER. EVERY DAY, EVERY HOUR THAT YOU LET IT GO UNCHECKED, IT TAKES DEEPER ROOT UNTIL YOU MAY BE OVERPOWERED BY IT — AND END UP DISTRUSTING ME. GO TO PRAYER THIS VERY DAY, AND ASK THE HOLY SPIRIT TO PLUCK OUT OF YOUR HEART ANY REMNANT OF BITTERNESS OR UNFOR-GIVENESS. I AM FAITHFUL TO RESTORE YOU."

Dearly Beloved: 19

PRAISE GOD FROM WHOM ALL BLESSINGS FLOW.

The Bible says, *"Faith cometh by hearing, and hearing by the Word of God" (Romans 10:17)*. The word "hearing" here includes the reading of God's Word and trusting in it without reservation.

As I sat down to write this, I heard the still, small voice of the Holy Spirit whisper to me that I could encourage many by setting before you a number of scriptural promises on which to anchor your faith.

I believe at least two of the following promises are especially for you at this particular time. Your two promises will seem to leap up in your heart, and you will know the Lord has sent you his Word for your specific situation:

- *"There shall none of my words be prolonged any more,*

but the word which I have spoken shall be done, saith the Lord God" *(Ezekiel 12:28)*.

• Here are two New Covenant promises: *"Behold, I will bring it health and cure, and I will cure them, and will reveal unto them the abundance of peace and truth" (Jeremiah 33:6). "And I will cleanse them from all their iniquity, whereby they have sinned against me; and I will pardon all their iniquities, whereby they have sinned, and whereby they have transgressed against me" (33:8).*

• *"When thou passest through the waters, I will be with thee; and through the rivers, they shall not overflow thee: when thou walkest through the fire, thou shalt not be burned; neither shall the flame kindle upon thee" (Isaiah 43:2).*

• *"Remember ye not the former things, neither consider the things of old. Behold, I will do a new thing; now it shall spring forth; shall ye not know it? I will even make a way in the wilderness, and rivers in the desert" (Isaiah 43:18-19).*

• *"Fear thou not; for I am with thee: be not dismayed; for I am thy God: I will strengthen thee; yea, I will help thee; yea, I will uphold thee with the right hand of my righteousness. Behold, all they that were incensed against thee shall be ashamed and confounded: they shall be as nothing; and they that strive with thee shall perish" (Isaiah 41:10-11).*

• *"He that hath a bountiful eye shall be blessed; for he giveth of his bread to the poor" (Proverbs 22:9).*

• *"Behold, the eye of the Lord is upon them that fear him, upon them that hope in his mercy; to deliver their soul from death, and to keep them alive in famine. Our soul waiteth for the Lord; he is our help and our shield. For our heart shall rejoice in him, because we have trusted in his holy name" (Psalm 33:18-21).*

May God speak to you through his precious Word.

Dearly Beloved: **20**

GOD BLESS AND KEEP YOU IN PEACE.

The Holy Spirit prompted me to read Exodus 12, which contains the account of Israel's deliverance from Egypt.

On the door of every Israelite home, the blood of a lamb was stricken on the two side-posts and lintel. This was to protect God's people from the passing angel of death. When the day came, a multitude of Israelites marched out of captivity, including 600,000 men plus women and children. *"The selfsame day...all the hosts of the Lord went out from the land of Egypt"* (Exodus 12:41).

In the next chapter, I stopped at verse 3, which reads: *"For by strength of hand the Lord brought you out from this place"* (13:3). God's people were delivered by the Lord's strength alone, not by human means.

David declares, *"God is my strength and power: and he maketh my way perfect... He sent from above, he took me; he drew me out of many waters; he delivered me from my strong enemy, and from them that hated me: for they were too strong for me... He is a buckler [protector] to all them that trust in him"* (2 Samuel 22:33, 17, 18, 31).

Our faith and strength may grow weak, but in our times of weakness God has given us marvelous promises to renew and strengthen us:

- *"Thou hast girded me with strength to battle"* (2 Samuel 22:40).

- *"They that stumbled are girded with strength"* (1 Samuel 2:4).

- *"The Lord will give strength unto his people; the Lord will bless his people with peace"* (Psalm 29:11).

• *"The God of Israel is he that giveth strength and power unto his people. Blessed be God"* (68:35).

• *"Forsake me not when my strength faileth... I will go in the strength of the Lord God"* (71:9, 16).

• *"Blessed is the man whose strength is in thee... They go from strength to strength, every one of them in Zion appeareth before God"* (84:5, 7).

Beloved, do you believe our God is strong? If he is strong, no power can stand before him. Therefore, commit everything into his mighty hand of strength and power. He will make a way. Most of all, believe this word: *"In the day when I cried you answeredst me, and strengthenedst me with strength in my soul"* (138:3).

God love and bless you.

Dearly Beloved: **21**

MAY THE PEACE OF GOD ABIDE IN YOU.

A Christian woman approached me some months ago with a rather emotional countenance and asked me if I had heard the latest news report. It was about an upheaval in Pakistan. "Can you believe what is happening?" she asked. "Every day is a bad-news day. Pakistan has nuclear capacity. Terrorists could take over and some mad Ayatollah could launch us into nuclear war." Shaking her head, she said, "I am really scared. Things are spinning out of control."

Right now, people are fearful all over the world. We are seeing the fulfillment of Jesus' warning, that a day would come when men's hearts fail for fear as they witness the things coming on the earth.

Those who have received my monthly messages know that in recent years I have cried out warnings about a coming housing crisis. I warned a crash was imminent. Yet I preached it with tears.

Now let me give you a clear word from God's heart, a word of encouragement. In spite of all the frightening news, God still has everything under control.

Here is the Word we believers must stand upon as the storm rages around us, words given to us by Jesus: *"Let not your heart be troubled, neither let it be afraid"* *(John 14:27)*. These are troubling times. But in such times the Word of God becomes our strength and hope.

• *"The Lord will be a refuge for the oppressed, a refuge in times of trouble. They that know thy name will put their trust in thee: for thou, Lord, hast not forsaken them that seek thee"* *(Psalm 9:9-10)*.

• *"In the time of trouble he shall hide me in his pavilion: in the secret of his tabernacle shall he hide me; he shall set me up upon a rock"* *(27:5)*.

I believe the most fearful, troubling days are still ahead. And I see nothing but growing despair for those who are not daily in God's Word and praying and talking to the Lord. It is his Word that lifts our spirits and produces faith. Discipline yourself now to open your Bible in the morning and start your day getting encouraged with his precious promises. Then talk to the Lord, even as you prepare for the day. Ask the Holy Spirit to strengthen your faith and hope.

There is one Scripture I repeat many times each day. I urge you also to claim it and believe it: *"Casting all your care upon him, for he careth for you"* *(1 Peter 5:7)*.

Dearly Beloved: 22

YOUR BATTLE IS THE LORD'S (see 2 Chronicles 20:15).

I am writing this to remind you the battle you are facing is not yours, but God's. If you are a child of his, you can be certain that Satan will "rage against you."

In 2 Chronicles 20, a great multitude came against God's people. King Jehoshaphat and his people set their hearts to seek the Lord and to fast. The king cried out to God a prayer that most of us have prayed at times in our spiritual journey: *"We have no might against these that come against us, neither do we know what to do; but our eyes are upon you"* (20:12). *"The Spirit of God came in the midst of the congregation...saying, Be not afraid nor dismayed...for the battle is not yours, but God's"* (20:14-15).

Isaiah gave this warning to all satanic forces: *"Whom have you reproached and blasphemed? And against whom have you exalted your voice?... Even against the Holy One of Israel"* (Isaiah 37:23).

God told his people Israel, and he tells us today: "The battle is not against you. It is Satan's rage against me, the Lord who abides in you." God said to Satan, *"I know where you abide, and where you come and go, and your rage against me"* (37:28).

I ask you: Where is your battle? In your marriage? Your business or job? Your finances? Your health? Does your battle get more intense day after day? If you have a heart for Jesus and a desire to cleave to him, you will face the rage of hell. But that is still not your battle.

You can end your battle quickly if you choose — simply by quitting and giving in to your fears and doubts. Satan will not bother those who give up their confidence in the Lord.

Yes, the battle is the Lord's, but we have a part — and that is to trust and believe his promises in the face of hopelessness and what seem to be impossibilities. *"Why sayest thou, O Jacob, and speakest, O Israel, My way is hid from the Lord, and my judgment is passed over from my God?"* (40:27).

Faith demands that I turn over all my problems — all my critical situations, all my fears, all my anxieties — into the hand of the Lord. When I have done all I can do and I know my battle is beyond my power, I must submit all into his hands.

Our Lord knows the raging of Satan, and we must truly believe he will act. He will bring us through floods and fires and put to chase all spiritual enemies. Here is God's Word concerning what he will do: *"Because of your rage against me...it has come into my ears, therefore I will put a hook in your nose, and my bridle in your lips, and I will turn you back by the way you came"* (37:29).

If you will hold fast to your faith — trusting him, resting in his promises, rejecting all lies of Satan coming into your mind — then expect God to come by his Spirit into your situation and bring an expected end to your particular battle. He will move heaven and earth to deliver you and make a way. The way out is to trust, trust, trust! *"He maketh wars to cease"* (Psalm 46:9).

Dearly Beloved: 23

WE EXALT THE NAME OF JESUS CHRIST OUR LORD!

Somebody reading this needs a touch from Jesus. When the Lord ministered here on earth, he went about healing and restoring the afflicted by simply touching them. When Jesus touched Peter's mother, "the fever left her." He touched the box casket of a dead boy, and the child came to life. He touched the eyes of blind people, and they could see. He touched the ear of a deaf man, who could suddenly hear. Parents brought their children to Jesus "that he should touch them." His gentle touch changed everything. Multitudes brought their sick and infirm, and Jesus took the time to reach out and touch them all, healing them.

If you truly know the Lord intimately, you have known and felt the touch of the hand of Jesus. In times of loneliness, times of discouragement, times of confusion, times so painful and uncertain, you cried out from the depth of your soul: "Lord Jesus, I need your touch. I need to feel your presence. Come, Jesus, and touch my thirsting soul."

Some need a touch of Jesus upon their mind. Satan has come with his wicked principalities to harass and overburden the mind with thoughts that are hellish — unbelieving thoughts, unChristlike thoughts, fearful thoughts, thoughts of unworthiness, thoughts of God's displeasure. Honest believers will tell you they have experienced these attacks on their mind. Satan is determined to destroy our faith and dependence on the Lord.

In Scripture, the touch of Jesus came in answer to a cry. There is no evidence he ever ignored or rejected such a cry. And he will not turn away from your cry but will mercifully respond to your need. In Matthew 8 we read of a leper coming to him, saying, *"Lord, if thou will, thou canst make me clean."* Jesus stretched out his hand and touched him, saying, *"I will; be thou clean. And immediately his leprosy was cleansed."*

Find a place alone with Jesus today, and say to him what the leper said: "Lord, you are able. Make me clean." Then expect that he who is no respecter of persons will touch and heal you, in mind, body, soul and spirit. The arm of the Lord is outstretched to you, but he waits for that cry of need, the cry for help that is also a cry of expectancy.

"And the Egyptians evil entreated us, and afflicted us, and laid upon us hard bondage; and when we cried unto the Lord God of our fathers, the Lord heard our voice, and looked on our affliction, and our labour, and our oppression: and the Lord brought us forth out of Egypt with a mighty hand, and with an outstretched arm, and with great terribleness, and with signs, and with wonders: and he hath brought us into this place, and hath given us this land, even a land that floweth with milk and honey" (Deuteronomy 26:6-9).

Dearly Beloved: 24

THE LOVE OF GOD FOR HIS PEOPLE NEVER FAILS.

While reading Psalm 13, I was impressed to send you a few words of encouragement I have gleaned from this blessed chapter.

David penned the words contained in this Psalm. He asked, "How long will you forget me, Lord? Forever? How long will you hide your face from me? How long shall I have sorrow in my heart daily? How long will the enemy be exalted over me?"

It sounds as if David felt that God had altogether left him to suffer, to wake up each day with a black cloud hanging over him. For a season, David spoke out of despair: "God, will this feeling of isolation go on forever? When will my prayers be answered?"

When troubles assail us though we know we love the Lord — when deliverance seems distant and hopeless — we sink under the pressure. Right now, someone reading these words is sinking under the awful pressure of a situation that seems to be unsolvable. They are on the verge of total despair, hoping a calm will come if only for a break in their trial.

In the midst of his own trial, David asked, "How long shall I take counsel in my soul?" He had formed one plan after another, trying to devise ways out of his trouble — but all his plans, all arrangements, had failed. Now he had nothing else to think of, no workable solution. He was at the end of it all.

How upsetting it is to see a ray of hope, a bit of sunshine, but then despair once again sets in. Keep in mind, this all happened to a godly man, someone after God's heart. David was a man who testified of having great trust in the Lord. Yet, like us, David went through hard times, as he describes in this Psalm.

How did David arise from this pit of despair? "I will trust in your mercy... I will sing."

Let me share with you reasons to keep trusting your way through your present trials:

• No matter how the storms may rage, our precious Lord will still be feeding the fowls of the air, dressing the lilies of the field, and supplying an ocean full of fish with their daily needs. "Your heavenly Father feedeth them..." Not one bird ever falls to the ground without the Father's eye upon it.

• What kind of Father would feed all the creatures of the earth and yet neglect his children? Jesus exhorted us to "give no thought" to everyday needs and problems, "for he careth for you."

Truly, the Lord loves you, and he will not turn a deaf ear to your cries. Hold on to his promises. Move on in faith. Wait on him patiently. He will never fail you.

Dearly Beloved: 25

IN CHRIST WE HAVE PEACE AND REST.

As I asked the Lord what I should share with you, I was

quickly led by the Holy Spirit to these verses in James 2:15-17: *"If a brother or sister be naked, and destitute of daily food, and one of you say unto them, Depart in peace, be ye warmed and filled; notwithstanding ye give them not those things which are needful to the body; what doth it profit? Even so faith, if it hath not works, is dead, being alone."*

These verses move me deeply. In my world travels, I have witnessed awful poverty and heartbreaking conditions in slums in South America and Africa especially. In Nairobi, Kenya, I walked through one of the largest slums on the continent. One and a quarter million impoverished people live there, in squalid tin shacks with no clean water, no electricity and open sewage ditches. The sights, the stench, the hunger are almost unbearable. It tears at your heart to see so many bony, sunken-cheeked children. You can never forget what you've seen; you are impacted for life.

I have always believed I am responsible for those needs that are placed before me, things I have seen with my own eyes. I did not cause the poverty and suffering; that is the result of man's fallen nature and lack of knowledge about the saving grace of Christ. But when hunger and nakedness and squalor are right there in front of my eyes, I am responsible to act — to do all in my ability and opportunity to provide hope and provisions. If I can't go there to serve in person, I can send others who are willing to sacrifice. I can help ministries that are already in place and doing these good works. Our ministry supports other works all over the world, in feeding, clothing, building shelters, schools and orphanages.

I hear it said, "We are not saved by good works." True, we are saved by faith alone, trusting in the sacrifice of Christ at Calvary. But good works testify to the compassion of Christ. And they echo the heart of God. It is obedience to the Word of the Lord to care for widows, the fatherless and the poor. Doing these things doesn't save me, but it does answer my need to stand one day before Christ and hear him say: *"I was hungry and you fed me, naked and you clothed me, in prison and you visited me. Insomuch as you have done it to one of these, the least of these, you have done it unto me"* (see Matthew 25:34-46).

James leaves no room for excuses. He says, "If you give them not those things needful to the body [those destitute of daily food], what doth it profit?" In other words, without good works, our faith has not profited. I judge no one, nor will I ever try to put guilt on anyone. But I know I have to do more than talk faith: I must act faith.

Dearly Beloved: 26

PRAISE GOD FOR HIS TENDER MERCIES.

I have a short message for those who are experiencing a painful, overwhelming situation. I am not speaking to those who now enjoy a time of rest from suffering, who are not in any kind of pain or sorrow. Thank God for those times of quiet rest.

Rather, I receive so many letters from precious followers of Jesus who are living with incredible inner sorrow and crisis situations: divorce, children on drugs or in jail, the death of a spouse. A woman who is so in love with the Lord grieves over the death of three of her children, who suffocated in a fire. A pastor grieves for his wife, who left him and his children for a lesbian lover. It goes on and on, as so many godly people are burdened with grief and pain.

I have a message for you who suffer sorrow, who grieve or live with pain. In Psalm 40, David cried, *"Innumerable evils* have compassed me about... Be pleased, O Lord, to deliver me: O Lord, make haste to help me" *(Psalm 40:12-13)*. "Let all those that seek you rejoice and be glad in thee... But I am poor and needy; the Lord thinketh upon me; thou art my help and my deliverer; do not tarry, O my Lord" *(40:16-17)*.

I have been so blessed and comforted by this one line in verse 17: *"The Lord thinketh upon me."* Imagine that. The Lord who created all things, the God of this universe, is thinking about me.

Even now, at this very hour, his thoughts are about you, in your hour of need.

When Israel was captive in Babylon, mourning over the loss of homes and families, enduring grief and trouble, God sent word to them through Jeremiah: *"For I know my thoughts that I think toward you, saith the Lord, thoughts of peace, and not evil, to give you an expected end" (Jeremiah 29:11)*. God said to his people, *"Your nightmare is going to end. I have only good, loving thoughts toward you, and if you seek me with all your heart, you will find me" (see 29:11-13)*.

God is not mad at you. Saintly people do get afflicted, so do not waver in your trust in him. In times of stress and feelings of loneliness and regrets, go to prayer. Pour your heart out to the Lord. He is thinking of you — and he is at work for you.

Dearly Beloved: 27

WE THANK GOD FOR HIS MANIFOLD MERCIES AND LOVINGKINDNESS.

I am led by the Holy Spirit to write to you about God opening shut doors. Someone reading this message will relate immediately to this, because you face one or more closed doors. There it is, right in your face, a door that seems to be continually locked. It could be a serious financial situation, and you've prayed for the door of some opportunity to open. Yet everything you try seems to fail; the doors simply don't open.

I don't know what your closed door may be, but for many it seems both the windows and doors of heaven are closed. The heavens seem as brass, and you can't seem to get through. This closed door I am speaking about is some issue, some situation, some need you've been praying much about. It may be a crisis that requires nothing less than a miracle. And you haven't yet received an answer to your fervent prayers and petitions to the Lord.

In Revelation, Christ refers to himself as *HE THAT OPENS AND SHUTS DOORS (see Revelation 3:7)*. This was in a letter sent to the believers in ancient Philadelphia, a church the Lord complimented for having kept the word of his patience and never denying his name. Simply put, in their most trying times, these people stood faithfully on God's Word. They did not accuse the Lord of neglecting them or turning a deaf ear to their cries.

Evidently, Satan had come against them with lies. His principalities and powers of darkness, lying spirits pouring out of the very bowels of hell, say that God has shut every door, that he isn't worthy of worship and faith. But these believers, whom Jesus said were of little strength, kept on trusting, waiting patiently for God to put the key in the door and open it. He holds the key to every shut door — and he alone sets before us open doors.

Here is what the Lord promised them, and it is our promise as well:

"Because you have kept the word of my patience [you did not give up in your trial], I also will keep you from the hour of

temptation which shall come upon all the world, to try them that dwell upon the earth" (3:10).

This hour of temptation is even now upon us. It holds incredible tests of faith so great and so fiery that many will fall into deadly unbelief. Indeed, a great falling away from enduring faith is now upon the whole world.

But you — because you still trust his promises, and are willing to die in faith even if you do not see the promises fulfilled — you will be kept from this worldwide temptation to fall into unbelief. God has heard your cry, and he knows the timing, the very hour, to open all doors. So, never give up. Never doubt. Stand on his promises. He will not fail you.

Dearly Beloved: **28**

TO GOD BE ALL PRAISE AND GLORY.

As I sat at my desk asking the Lord how I could bless you, I was moved simply to give you something from his Word.

I offer the following Scriptures, trusting that at least one of them will be a word just for you. I know God is faithful to send us a special word when we so need it. And I believe there is something here especially for you.

1. Psalm 32:6-8: *"For this shall every one that is godly pray unto thee in a time when thou mayest be found: surely in the floods of great waters they shall not come nigh unto him. Thou art my hiding place; thou shalt preserve me from trouble; thou shalt compass me about with songs of deliverance. I will instruct thee and teach thee in the way which thou shalt go: I will guide thee with mine eye."*

2. Psalm 31:6-8: *"I have hated them that regard lying vanities: but I trust in the Lord. I will be glad and rejoice in thy* mercy: for thou hast considered my trouble; thou hast known my soul in adversities; and hast not shut me up into the hand of the enemy: thou hast set my feet in a large room."

3. Psalm 41:1-3: *"Blessed is he that considereth the poor: the Lord will deliver him in time of trouble. The Lord will preserve him, and keep him alive; and he shall be blessed upon the earth: and thou wilt not deliver him unto the will of his enemies. The Lord will strengthen him upon the bed of languishing: thou wilt make all his bed in his sickness."*

4. Psalm 31:1, 5: *"In thee, O Lord, do I put my trust; let me never be ashamed: deliver me in thy righteousness.... Into thine hand I commit my spirit: thou hast redeemed me, O Lord God of truth."*

5. Psalm 56:8, 9, 11: *"Thou tellest my wanderings: put thou my tears into thy bottle: are they not in thy book? When I cry unto thee, then shall mine enemies turn back: this I know; for God is for me. In God have I put my trust: I will not be afraid what man can do unto me."*

6. Psalm 86:17: *"Show me a token for good; that they which hate me may see it, and be ashamed: because thou, Lord, hast helped me, and comforted me."*

7. Psalm 88:1-3: *"O Lord God of my salvation, I have cried day and night before thee: let my prayer come before thee: incline thine ear unto my cry, for my soul is full of troubles: and my life draweth nigh unto the grave."*

Please underline the Scripture portion that the Spirit witnesses is yours. Believe it! God has sent it to you today.

Dearly Beloved: **29**

GOD GIVES STRENGTH TO THE WEAK.

The Holy Spirit has prompted me to speak to you about thanksgiving. The Hebrew root word for thanksgiving is "adoration." The apostle Paul wrote, *"Giving thanks always for all things unto God and the Father in the name of our Lord Jesus Christ"* (Ephesians 5:20).

The longer I live and the closer I get to the end of my race here on earth, the more I feel the need to adore the Lord by thanking him in all things. *"In every thing give thanks: for this is the will of God in Christ Jesus concerning you"* (1 Thessalonians 5:18).

Giving thanks — in all things? In everything? Yes, in sickness and in health. In good times and in bad. In storms and in sunshine. David said, *"Let us come before his presence with thanksgiving"* (Psalm 95:2). All too often we do not come into the Lord's presence with thanksgiving. Instead, we come to him burdened down with our problems, failing to give him thanks for keeping us in so many ways. The truth is, not one true lover of the Lord can say God has ever failed him.

I ask you, when was the last time you stopped everything to offer thanks to the Lord for what he has done for you? *"O give thanks unto the Lord; call upon his name: make known his deeds among the people. Sing unto him, sing psalms unto him: talk ye of all his wondrous works"* (105:1-2).

I give thanks to the Lord for all his wondrous works that we have witnessed throughout the past year. And now I give thanks for what he is going to do through the coming year.

Dearly Beloved: 30

GREETINGS IN THE WONDERFUL NAME OF THE LORD.

I have been meditating for the past few days on Psalms 142 and 143. I recommend you take the time to read these powerful Psalms to encourage your faith.

I was interested in what David was going through when he said, *"When my spirit was overwhelmed in me, then you knew my path"* (142:3). He repeats this in 143:4, *"My spirit is overwhelmed in me; my heart within me is desolate."* David is actually saying to God, "I am drowning in trouble. I am under attack by my enemies. It is bringing me low." He cried to the Lord, *"Hear my cry, for I am brought very low... Bring my soul out of this prison"* (142:6-7).

Beloved, these words are written for our sake, for our instruction. Here is encouragement for all of God's people who are overwhelmed by troubles and afflictions. Some are drowning in financial troubles, overwhelmed with debt. Multitudes of precious believers can hardly make ends meet. Many widows and elderly couples are barely making it.

Often I have been accused of being too gloomy, too negative. People say nobody wants to hear bad news, that they turn off any preacher who talks about pain, suffering and troubles. But the truth is, most of us live in a world where life can be absolutely overwhelming at times. Like David, we face a flood of troubles; we are afflicted even in our righteousness. We endure sickness, death of loved ones, times of confusion, not knowing what to do next. We face hellish attacks of Satan against our faith.

It is in our overwhelming times we learn to seek God and learn to cry out in our pain. David said, *"I poured out my complaint before him, I showed before him my trouble"* (142:2). *"In thy faithfulness answer me"* (143:1). Are you even now overwhelmed by circumstances in your life? Do what David did:

• *"I stretch forth my hands unto thee: my soul thirsts after thee, as a thirsty land"* (143:6).

• *"Hide not your face from me... Cause me to hear your lovingkindness in the morning; for in thee do I trust: cause me to know the way wherein I should walk; for I lift up my soul to you"* (143:7-8).

• *"Deliver me, O Lord, from my enemies: I flee to you to hide me. Teach me to do your will; for thou art my God: thy spirit is good; lead me into the land of uprightness. Quicken me, O Lord, for thy name's sake: for thy righteousness' sake bring my soul out of trouble"* (143:9-11).

Be encouraged. God has everything under control! He will meet your need right on time.

Dearly Beloved: 31

MAY THE PEACE OF GOD RULE IN YOUR HEART.

The Spirit has been making it so clear to me that all my praying is totally in vain unless I pray in faith. I could weep, fast, intercede, agonize and travail in prayer, yet make no impact with the Lord at all — unless I was doing it all with simple, childlike faith.

God will not act on our behalf without faith. The Word says, *"Let not that man [the doubter] think he shall receive anything from God"* (James 1:7).

The Lord commands us to trust him. Yet often we have so little confidence in him, so little faith in his willingness and desire to answer our heart-cry. When we get to heaven, we will be amazed to discover all the blessings, peace and power we had at our disposal but did not appropriate because of our weak faith.

I AM GREATLY MOVED UPON BY THE HOLY SPIRIT TO CHALLENGE YOU TO INCREASE YOUR FAITH. Ask the Lord to forgive your unbelief and to flood your soul with confidence in his willingness to over-answer your sincere prayers.

Do you want an increase in faith? When you go to prayer again, use the following Scriptures to reason with the Lord. He will not deny his own Word. Lay hold upon these:

• Psalm 62:8 • Psalm 91:4 • Psalm 56:3 • Proverbs 30:5 • Jeremiah 29:10-14

Hold on by faith! He will answer you and soon.

Dearly Beloved: 32

GREETINGS IN CHRIST'S PRECIOUS NAME.

Just as I was preparing to write this message, the Holy Spirit spoke clearly to me: "Edify the people. Bless them with my Word." I responded, "Lord, I would love to, but what do you want me to say? You must impress deeply upon my spirit the right word for these times."

Here is what I received from the Lord. I hope you will receive it and be truly edified. Perhaps you are the very one whom God has prepared to receive such a word of encouragement at this particular time:

• God desires that you believe what he has spoken to you, especially about healing and guidance. (See John 4:48-50.)

Jesus told a nobleman his son was going to be healed. *"The man believed the word that Jesus had spoken unto him, and he went his way."* This man believed the Lord's word, and his son was healed that same hour.

• The Lord is going to answer your heart-cry according to the multitude of his tender mercies. His timing is perfect, so be patient. (See Psalm 69:13-14, 16-18, 32-33.)

In this passage you must substitute "demonic power" for "enemies." Your real enemy is Satan, who hates your continued hunger for a closer walk with the Lord.

• Here is a very specific word for you personally. Yes, a number of people will receive this same word in my message here, but the Holy Spirit has a way of applying God's Word in different ways to many believers.

Go to Psalm 145. Before you read it, pray that the Holy Spirit will speak to you directly in a verse or two. I know the Lord spoke this to my heart, that you are going to be edified in Psalm 145.

(Verse 14 is one that has been pinpointed to me for you, but the Spirit may pinpoint others to you also.)

May God give you much Holy Ghost fight to resist the devil and put him to flight.

(Note: The following message was written in the days following the attacks on the Twin Towers at the World Trade Center on September 11, 2001.)

Dearly Beloved:

THE LORD BE PRAISED.

The rubble from the Twin Towers is still burning, and this city is still on alert status. The people still cry when they look south and see only empty space where the proud towers once stood and where thousands of people remain buried. Yet, slowly, New York is getting back to a semblance of normalcy.

The fire station two blocks from Times Square Church lost fifteen firemen in the calamity. Last week, my wife Gwen presented the station with a large wreath, and Pastor Carter Conlon handed the fire chief a check for $350,000 for the widows' and children's fund. We also presented the local police station with a gift of $350,000 for their widows' and children's fund. These funds were sent to us by caring friends and supporters of our ministry from all over the world. It looks like the total will exceed one million dollars. Thanks to all who gave, unsolicited by us.

We did not want these particular funds to be lost in any red tape, so we designated it all to meet the local needs of hurting families. The funds are being dispersed immediately to pay for the desperate needs of those waiting for other help. Every dollar received has gone directly to families who came to us in great need, and to the New York Police and Firemen Widows' and Children's Funds.

We saw officers and firemen wipe tears from their eyes when we handed them the checks. It was also deeply touching to see children bringing in piggy banks and shoeboxes full of money they had collected. Hour by hour, people came, including young children, piling up banks of flowers, thank-you notes and letters.

Since the bombing, Times Square Church has been packed. The young people here are experiencing a marvelous revival, with many being saved. Our prayer rooms are filled with seekers on Sundays, and many are coming to Christ throughout the week.

We at Times Square Church were warned thirty days before the attack of impending national calamity. Strong prophetic warnings were sounded publicly. When the crisis came, we were the first church on the scene, distributing food, water, boots, gloves, goggles, eye drops and other requested equipment.

We have been warning America from our pulpit, pleading prophetically, but we also rushed to Ground Zero in time of need. We weep with those who weep, but we did not miss the message God has given America through this disaster.

God bless and keep you.

Dearly Beloved: 34

GOD HAS EVERYTHING UNDER CONTROL.

Yesterday, September 19, I stood at Ground Zero — just yards away from the burning rubble of the former Twin Towers. It looks like a devastated war zone: closed parking lots filled with unclaimed cars covered with inches of dirt and dust. Huge buildings nearby that will have to come down. Blocks and blocks of shuttered businesses. Smashed cars and trucks bulldozed into piles. Rows of refrigerated trucks where rescue workers were bringing body parts for temporary storage. You can literally feel a frightful sense of judgment as you walk through such indescribable destruction and death.

Our ministry was one of the first on the scene, right at the site. Our workers were there night and day, alongside the Red

Cross, supplying food, water and essential supplies to the police, firemen and volunteers.

So far we have knowledge of only one lost from our congregation, the son of one of our staff members. We have heard incredible testimonies of deliverance by our congregation.

Yesterday, standing before the smoldering, five-story-high pile of rubble, I cried inwardly, "Oh Lord, if every American could stand here and behold this awful destruction, they would come to the only possible conclusion: you are warning this nation to repent."

Times Square Church was forewarned by the Lord that a calamity was coming weeks before it happened. A month prior, our leadership was impressed by the Holy Spirit to cancel all special speakers and scheduled meetings. We canceled our missions convention and citywide youth rallies. We shut things down and called the congregation to prayer.

We have experienced an unusual visitation of the Holy Spirit as a result. God's Spirit suddenly moved in, and a holy quiet fell on the house. On one occasion, we sat in total silence for over an hour. People spoke in hushed tones. There was soft weeping, with people coming forward and kneeling, reaching out to the Lord. These are the manifestations of a Holy Ghost visitation: a holy, awesome silence, and weeping and fervent prayer in every service. The Holy Spirit revealed to us that the divine silence in our meetings was a preparation for the trying times ahead.

Dearly Beloved: 35

REJOICE IN THE LORD AND BE GLAD!

In the book of Jude, we read of a future day so wicked and

vile, God will come with ten thousands of his saints to execute judgment for all ungodly deeds. Jude prophesied men would be given over to their filthy lusts, becoming mockers, sensual, *"foaming out their own shame"* (Jude 13). These would comprise a society of corrupt fornicators going after "strange flesh," referring to pandemic homosexuality.

Today, America is not the only nation casting aside all moral restraint. The moral landslide is worldwide, and it is becoming very evident that Satan is retching the abominations of hell upon humankind. It is a time, we are warned in Scripture, when the devil will try to seduce God's elect.

Jude looked ahead into those awful, wicked times and saw something else, something most inspiring and miraculous. In the midst of all the immorality and mounting degradation, he witnessed a people *"sanctified by God the Father, and preserved in Jesus Christ, and called"* (Jude 1).

No matter how corrupt this world becomes in the days ahead — no matter how devilish the media, TV and movies become, no matter how much devil worship increases, no matter how far homosexuals force their agenda on society, no matter if the devil himself walks our streets — God is going to preserve his children. He is going to preserve for himself a sanctified, holy people. He will keep them from the wicked one, and they will become strong in faith and devotion, while the ungodly race toward destruction.

Hear the word of the Lord: *"The very God of peace sanctify you wholly; and I pray God your whole spirit and soul and body be preserved blameless unto the coming of our Lord Jesus Christ. Faithful is he that calleth you, who also will do it"* (1 Thessalonians 5:23-24).

David said, *"The Lord forsaketh not his saints; they are preserved for ever"* (Psalm 37:28). *"When the wicked walk on every side...thou shalt keep them, O Lord, thou shalt preserve them from this generation for ever"* (12:7-8).

Let this prayer of the apostle Paul be yours and mine in the evil, troubled times ahead: *"The Lord shall deliver me from every evil work, and preserve me unto his heavenly kingdom"* (2 Timothy 4:18).

Rejoice! God has covenanted to keep and preserve those who fully trust him.

Dearly Beloved: 36

MAY GOD GIVE YOU PEACE AND REST IN YOUR HEART.

I believe in miracles!

There is a mother in our church choir who has been praying for her son for years. He had fallen deep into sin as a teenager. She prayed, "God, whatever it takes, save him." Instead of turning to Christ, he became a Muslim. For the next seven years, he buried himself in that devilish doctrine. But his mother kept praying. Islam sent the boy into a deep depression. In his awful despair, he jumped from a six-story building, hoping to kill himself. Instead, he landed on his feet, crushing a number of bones — and he survived. Last Sunday, he limped onto our stage and told how Jesus Christ miraculously saved him. His mother sat in the choir, praising God and remembering her many tears and hours in prayer. God heard her cry.

Thank God for miracles today!

A teenage boy in our church spoke of praying that God would

use him in his high school, which is located near Ground Zero and the demolished Twin Towers. He and a friend began to stand outside the school every day, praying out loud. Some mocked them, but others began to join them. It led to the school permitting them to conduct Bible classes in the school. The young man is so overjoyed, and now some teachers are attending. He said, "Can you imagine God using a scared little nobody like me? God still does miracles."

Thank God, he is still the miracle worker!

A young man in prison wrote us a letter that moved me deeply. Talk about miracles! Here is what he wrote, word for word:

"David, I receive your sermons through the mail. I am one of the school shooters. I'm the one they blame for starting it all off. On October 1, 1997, I went into Pearl High School and killed two students and wounded seven. I also killed my mother before this. After I came to jail I got saved. If there is any way that I can help your ministry, I would love to. Maybe I could give you my testimony. I'll do anything to help. I look forward to your sermons each month..."

Yes, I believe in miracles!

Dearly Beloved: *37*

GRACE BE UNTO YOU AND PEACE FROM GOD OUR FATHER.

I have been questioned as to why so many of my recent messages have focused on mercy, reconciliation and hope. Some people have expressed concern that I may have turned from preaching repentance and holiness. Not so.

When I traveled as an evangelist, I never got to know the people I preached to. I was never in one place long enough to discover all the hurts, needs and burdens of God's people. But now, as a pastor, I hear firsthand of all the troubles and trials endured by those in the congregation at Times Square Church, as well as churches around the world.

Beloved, I have discovered that GOD'S PEOPLE ARE HURTING DEEPLY. They are being tempted and tried and tossed about by great adversities and needs. The problems in families are overwhelming. Many sheep are groaning in misery and pain — hurting, thirsty, spiritually crippled, living from crisis to crisis.

GOD HAS MADE IT CLEAR TO ME I CANNOT CLUB HURTING SHEEP. INSTEAD, TENDER MERCY IS NEEDED. Even the fiery prophet Jeremiah cried, *"O Lord, correct me, but with justice; not in thine anger, lest thou bring me to nothing"* *(Jeremiah 10:24)*. Jeremiah was saying, "Lord, be tender with me, because I am in no condition to hear anger or wrath, or I'll be reduced to nothing."

God will never use his word to reduce you to nothing when you are hurting. All he asks of his people is a repentant, broken spirit. He responds with mercy to our crying need.

Rest in his mercy and love, for he pities his children.

Dearly Beloved: 38

I PRAY YOU ARE ENJOYING THE PRESENCE OF THE LORD.

There is a text in the original Hebrew that has blessed me greatly, and I want to share it with you. *"When designing pursuers approached me, who are far from thy law; then you, O Jehovah, wast near with all thy faithful commandments"* *(Psalm 119:150-151, Helen Spurrell Translation)*.

Demonic principalities and powers had surrounded David, trying to bring him and Israel to ruin and destruction. Yet this man of God testified that as the enemy drew near, he trusted the Lord to draw even nearer. David said that God held him by his right hand, walking him through every enemy assault.

Here in David's testimony is a wonderful promise for you and me. We can be sure Satan is out to destroy, harass and pull down all who love the Lord. The enemy will do all within his power to bring us into a pit of despair, confusion, guilt and condemnation.

Do you have any satanic, "designing pursuers" coming against you right now? Overwhelming temptations? Trials? Financial burdens? Marriage or family problems? Business problems? When your pursuers come near you with a design to destroy you, take heart: the Lord God Almighty is even nearer. He is at your side — and if he is near you, he will act on your behalf. I cannot imagine God being near any child of his and yet sitting by allowing the devil to abuse or corrupt his beloved in any way.

Read Psalm 68:1-4 and see what God has promised to do for you, if you will but trust him. You can claim these four verses for now and throughout the year. Memorize these verses, stand on them, and God will put your enemies to chase.

Dearly Beloved: 39

THE LORD BLESS AND KEEP YOU.

I pray diligently over these messages, and while praying about what the Lord would have me write in this one, the Holy Spirit whispered clearly: "Encourage God's people. Tell them how much they are loved by the Lord and how greatly he delights in his children."

I believe this is a special word for many reading this message. You need to hear deep within, at this very hour, that the Lord is going to keep you, and that in your present hour of testing he delights in you. Here is the text I believe you need to receive as a personal word from him right now:

"Despise not the chastening of the Lord; neither be weary of his correction: for whom the Lord loveth he correcteth; even as a father the son in whom he delighteth" (Proverbs 3:11-12).

Even if what you are going through right now is loving discipline, remember it is a sure sign your Father loves you and delights in you. If you will receive this word — that he deeply loves you and rejoices over you — you will know all things are working out for your good, and that your steps are truly being ordered by him.

(Note: The following message was written during the early years of Times Square Church in New York City.)

Dearly Beloved: 40

SATAN HAS NO RIGHT TO HARASS YOU AND YOUR FAMILY. TRUST GOD FOR YOUR DELIVERANCE!

God releases his awesome delivering power to those who completely trust him. Those who "stagger" in faith, fretting and worrying, will never be delivered from the snare of Satan.

The answer is simple, yet many of us just don't get it. We go on living in turmoil and fear, while at our fingertips are all the precious promises needed to set us free from crises in this life. God hates our unbelief, mostly because it ties his hands and keeps us from enjoying his glorious provision. Make it a priority each day to pray, "Lord, help my unbelief. Give me childlike trust in you."

WE COULD NOT GO ON HERE IN NEW YORK CITY WITHOUT COMPLETE TRUST IN THE LORD. The problems are too overwhelming. Millions of people are living in overcrowded conditions. The city is going wild with violence, drugs, murder, a new strain of TB that is airborne, and the plague of AIDS.

Our workers who minister every day to the diseased street people and homeless who carry these diseases are not afraid. They trust the Lord to protect them and to strengthen them in this work.

I thank God for allowing us to be his channels in raising up a thriving church on Broadway, with thousands of lives being touched. But we did not come to New York City simply to build a church. We came to do what Jesus would have done: to minister to the poor, the hungry, the homeless, the addicted, the worst among sinners.

We rejoice that God is enabling us to bring Christ's redeeming gospel to many who once were considered hopeless by every human measure. A small army has already been saved from the streets, and every day more and more are being rescued.

GOD IS PROVING HIS POWER OVER ALL THE DESTRUCTIVE FORCES OF HELL. And he will show his power on your behalf, too, in the trial you are facing. Amen!

Dearly Beloved: 41

GOD HAS NEVER, EVER FAILED US.

No matter what happens to the economy, no matter what

crisis we face, no matter what sorrow or trouble may come our way — OUR BLESSED LORD IS LEADING AND CARING FOR US EVERY STEP OF THE WAY.

God had to finally disown those he delivered out of Egypt, because they doubted and limited him after having been so miraculously coddled in his loving arms. It isn't simply that God would like for us to trust him in difficult times — he demands it. This is why Scripture so strongly warns us against unbelief. We are told it grieves the Lord and shuts us off from every blessing and good work he has promised. Our unbelief makes every promise "of no effect."

For us in New York City, this is not a dead theology. We have to practice what we preach just to survive each day. If we did not fully trust the Lord's promises and rely on Jesus with all that is in us, we would freeze up with fear and panic. In certain areas, the streets are like war zones; people live in constant fear and danger, and bystanders are murdered left and right. Our costs to care for those we minister to are heavy, and the needs of hurting people are so enormous. IF WE DID NOT REST IN GOD'S STEADFAST PROMISES, WE WOULD BE OVERWHELMED.

But we are not overwhelmed — we are not afraid. As the problems grow worse, we grow stronger in the power of the Holy Spirit.

Dearly Beloved: 42

REJOICE — YOU HAVE A COMFORTER!

While sitting down to write this, I was powerfully impressed by the Holy Spirit to bring the following word to you:

"In this year, you are going to need the ministry of the Holy Spirit more than ever before. There is coming an acceleration of events far more amazing and frightful than all the changes of the previous year [1991]. Learn to acknowledge the presence of the Holy Ghost; talk to him frequently; wait before the Lord until you hear his voice. He desires to be your guide, your help in need, your entire and complete source of strength, peace and comfort.

"If God is with you , why be afraid? Who can harm you? Who can resist His power? Is God with you? He is if you love Him and walk in His truth. So let not your heart be troubled or afraid. We are all being tested in our faith — and God has everything under control."

Dearly Beloved: *43*

I know Jesus loves the poor, the widows, and the fatherless — and he has given us a loving commandment to feed and clothe them and to preach to them the gospel. In over fifty years of ministry to the needy in New York City, I have learned a few things I would like to share with you:

1. Compassion and sympathy are not the same thing. Many Christians get emotionally stirred over poverty, homelessness and other such pressing needs — but often it is only a fleeting sympathy. Compassion, in order to be sustained, cannot be primarily emotional. I believe compassion is simply doing what Jesus said to do — often without tears or heartrending emotion. Sometimes those emotions can be a drain on the spirit. Our ministry feeds hundreds daily...we take in addicts, prostitutes, alcoholics, widows and single mothers...and we do it all joyfully, with a smile. We are not motivated by guilt or condemnation. Jesus said to do it, so we simply do it.

2. Our giving to the poor, homeless and destitute ought not to be spasmodic or emotional. We should not have our emotions ravaged by pictures or stories of starving children and emaciated human beings. Tears don't last very long; "emotions of the hour" wear away eventually, and the true burden vanishes. Rather than relying on our emotions, we need to make giving toward human needs a regular, systematic part of our Christian walk.

3. When our ministry workers call upon companies to donate food and clothing to help us reach the poor in New York City, they don't do it with tears. They aren't just praying about the needs before us — they're doing diligent work to meet those needs, systematically and joyfully without being drained by emotions.

4. IT'S THAT SIMPLE. Jesus said we are to "feed the hungry, clothe the naked, bring into our homes the homeless, visit the prisoners" — so we simply do it. We are called to support his work of love to the destitute, so we do it.

And we do it all with no thought of reward. There is no self-examination of whether we care deeply enough, no wondering whether we have the proper kind of compassion. We just do it, period. We believe this is Jesus' way for all his servants.

Dearly Beloved: 44

GREETINGS IN CHRIST TO ALL THE SAINTS WHO RECEIVE THIS MESSAGE.

There is much fear and anxiety in our nation today about the future. There is a shaking taking place, in God's house and in our society. Condoms are being distributed in our schools, even to eighth and ninth graders, without the consent of parents. Our nation's moral values are collapsing right before our eyes.

There is a growing cynicism in America — a loss of trust in government leaders, a feeling of being betrayed by pastors and evangelists — and a cry is being heard everywhere now: "Who can we trust?"

God warned us he is going to shake everything that can be shaken, and the only things left standing will be those which are truly of him. Two results will evolve from all the turbulence:

1. The ungodly will cry out for a strong leader, just as Russia did. The stage is being set for the rise of the Antichrist.

2. Devoted followers of Jesus will cast themselves totally on the Lord as their only hope and confidence. David wrote, *"It is better to take refuge in the Lord, than to trust in man"* (Psalm 118:8). David also said the faithful servant of God *"shall not be afraid of evil tidings; his heart is fixed, trusting in the Lord"* (112:7).

If David were living today, I believe he would lift his voice and cry out to God's people once more, *"Ye that fear the Lord, trust in him. He is your shield and protector"* (115:11).

I still believe more than ever that THE CHURCH'S GREATEST HOUR IS STILL AHEAD. Right now there is a new generation of young ministers rising up in the land who are godly, humble, broken in spirit, steeped in God's Word, and free of all materialistic baggage of the past. These devoted young leaders are not interested in numbers, bigness, hype, entertainment or fame. They have been sickened by ministries and preachers who are centered on self and money.

I thank God for them. And I thank him there is great hope!

Dearly Beloved:

GOD IS FAITHFUL AT ALL TIMES.

Gwen and I recently spoke to a godly woman who has reached the end of her endurance. This woman's family has seen incredible suffering. She wakes up each day with a black cloud of pain hanging over her home. She has spent endless hours praying and calling on the Lord for help, and her friends have stood with her in intercession.

But month after month goes by and things do not change. Just when she sees a ray of hope, things go back to the way they were, yet everything is worse. She hears a message or reads something that inspires her faith and she tries to soldier on. But now she is totally worn out. She cries a lot. She can hardly sleep. She is far beyond asking why there is so much endless suffering and pain. Now she is simply hoping to see a little light at the end of her dark tunnel of sorrow.

She told us, "I have come to the place where I feel I have the right to give up. I've done everything God has asked me. I have believed, I have sought him, I have been faithful in church and in reading his Word. Yet I see no relief. I feel alone and helpless, depressed. I am numb because of the constant nagging thought that things will only get worse in spite of all my efforts to obey. Now I have to fight this thought: 'I have a right to feel as I do because I see no end to suffering.'"

We are praying diligently for her and her family. We believe she will not faint in the battle and that the Lord will send her help and encouragement. But what she has said in her despair truly touches something deep inside my soul. Many godly believers have come to the same place of hopelessness, and in sorrow they also cry, "I have a right to quit the fight. I have a right to be angry. I have a right to question God. When will he answer my cry? Has the Lord passed me by?"

In Job's despair, he cried, *"(He) has destroyed me on every side, and I am gone: and my hope hath (he) removed like a tree... He counts me as one of his enemies" (Job 19:10-11). Job then added: "He has fenced me in so I cannot pass, and he has set darkness in my paths" (19:8).*

Does any of this sound familiar to you? Is this your battle? Is it the struggle of someone you know? Beloved, God is merciful. He will not turn from you in your trial. He will not hold it against you for expressing such thoughts when you are down and hurting. Job came out of his trial to a place of hope, and so will you.

"I go forward, but he is not there: and backward, but I cannot perceive him: on the left hand, where he does work, but I cannot behold him: he hides himself on the right hand, I cannot see him. But he knows the way that I take; when he has tried me, I shall come forth as gold" (23:8-10).

Dearly Beloved: 46

CHRIST REIGNS!

Often people write to us saying, "I have no one to talk to, no one to share my burden with. Nobody has time to hear my cry. I need someone I can pour my heart out to."

King David was surrounded by people. He was married, with a large family, and had many companions at his side. Yet we hear the same cry even from David: "To whom shall I go?" It is in our very nature to want another human being, with a face, eyes and ears, to listen to us and advise us.

When Job became overwhelmed by his trials, he cried out with grief: *"Oh that one would hear me!"* (Job 31:35). He uttered this cry while sitting before his so-called friends. Yet those friends had no sympathy for Job's troubles. Instead, they were messengers of despair.

In his sorrow, Job turned only to the Lord: *"Behold, my witness is in heaven, and my record is on high… Mine eye poureth tears unto God"* (16:19-20). In the Psalms, David urged God's people to do likewise: *"Trust in him at all times; ye people, pour out your heart before him: God is a refuge for us"* (Psalm 62:8). David also wrote in Psalm 142:

"I cried unto the Lord with my voice; with my voice unto the Lord did I make my supplication. I poured out my complaint before him; I shewed before him my trouble. When my spirit was overwhelmed within me, then thou knewest my path. In the way wherein I walked have they privily laid a snare for me. I looked on my right hand, and beheld, but there was no man that would know me: refuge failed me; no man cared for my soul. I cried unto thee, O Lord: I said, Thou art my refuge and my portion in the land of the living" (142:1-5).

I believe in my heart this message is an invitation to you from the Holy Spirit to find a private place where you can frequently pour out your soul to the Lord. David "poured out his complaint," and so can you. You can speak to Jesus about everything — your problems, your present trial, your finances, your health — and tell him how overwhelmed you are, even how discouraged you are. He will hear you with love and sympathy, and he will not despise your cry.

God answered David. He answered Job. And for centuries he has answered the heart-cry of everyone who has trusted his promises. Likewise, he has promised to hear you and guide you. Indeed, he has pledged by oath to be your strength. Go to him, and you will come out renewed.

Dearly Beloved: 47

THE LORD IS MERCIFUL AND GOOD TO THOSE WHO TRUST HIM.

While I was praying about this message, the Holy Spirit whispered to me: "SOMEBODY READING THIS IS IN NEED OF ENCOURAGEMENT. SOMEBODY NEEDS TO BE REFRESHED AND DELIVERED FROM MENTAL AND PHYSICAL PAIN AND CONFUSION. SOMEBODY NEEDS A SPECIAL WORD OF HOPE EVEN WHILE READING THIS."

Is that somebody you? I am thinking of someone who is facing trouble on all sides, someone nearly overwhelmed by fears within and fightings without. Most likely this person has no one to talk to who would fully understand, no one to trust in such an hour of trial.

I know in my spirit that God is using my pen right now to bring a word of hope and refreshment to someone near the end of their patience and endurance. Please hear the word of the Lord as I write this to you under the anointing of the Holy Spirit. God has heard your cry, and the following words to you are from his loving heart:

Satan is trying to implant lies in your mind in your time of weakness and trouble. He will try to convince you God is not with you. If you believe that lie, you can never escape Satan's trap.

If you will quiet yourself before the Lord, and call on him in secret prayer, the Holy Spirit will tell you clearly: God is with you. He has not forsaken you. He sees you and knows what you are suffering. Jesus said, *"Lo, I am with you always, even unto the end of the world"* (Matthew 28:20).

You are loved, and you are needed. Satan is a liar, hoping you will give in to despair by believing you are alone in your struggle. No, you are not alone — not ever. God has someone praying for you in your time of need.

You are going to come out of your trial victorious. But you must believe God has heard your cry. Just lean on the Lord. If he could show you all the good things ahead for you, you would rejoice with gladness.

Finally, hear God's heart through his pure Word:

"For I know the thoughts that I think toward you, saith the Lord, thoughts of peace, and not of evil, to give you an expected end. Then shall ye call upon me, and ye shall go and pray unto me, and I will hearken unto you. And ye shall seek me, and find me, when ye shall search for me with all your heart" (Jeremiah 29:11-13).

Dearly Beloved: 48

As I was in prayer, the Holy Spirit spoke to my heart about four expectations that God's people should trust him to bring to pass. These expectations are based on absolute promises the Lord has made to us. Our God is a promise-maker and a promise-keeper!

1. EXPECT TO BE REWARDED AS YOU DILIGENTLY SEEK THE LORD. *"God is a rewarder of them that diligently seek him"* (Hebrews 11:6).

You can ask in faith for a token from the Lord to encourage and rekindle your confidence. God is always on time, and he knows you need a ray of hope and good news in your time of testing. Expect him to keep his promise to reward you now, when you are in greatest need. God cannot lie — he has said he rewards those who diligently seek him — so seek him daily. And truly believe this will be your season of great spiritual blessing.

2. EXPECT TO SEE EVIDENCE OF A PROGRESSIVE MIRACLE IN YOUR LIFE. *"With God all things are possible"* *(Mark 10:27)*.

I have written about instantaneous miracles and progressive miracles. Progressive miracles start in unseen, quiet ways and unfold little by little, one small mercy at a time. You are now in such a miracle. Expect to see God working in mysterious ways, unseen to the human eye. This should be the season you can say, "I don't know how it will come to pass — I don't see much happening right now — but I believe God set into motion an answer to my prayers the very first hour I asked."

3. EXPECT TO ENTER INTO GOD'S PROMISED PLACE OF REST. *"There remaineth therefore a rest to the people of God...enter into that rest"* *(Hebrews 4:9, 11)*.

The recent year has been one of the most stressful for many believers. It was a year of incredible calamities, problems and trials. Now the Lord desires that you trust him to bring you into his promised rest. God never intended for his children to live in fear and despair. We need a reckless faith, a trust in him in the face of fear and trouble. Now is the time to lay it all on Jesus.

4. EXPECT THE HOLY SPIRIT TO BE ALWAYS "IN HIS TEMPLE." *"Know ye not that your body is the temple of the Holy Spirit"* *(1 Corinthians 6:19)*.

The Holy Spirit abides in the heart of every believer. He is omnipresent throughout the world and universe. I face each day acknowledging that he is here in his temple to comfort and guide me, encourage and anoint me, to reveal the glory of Jesus Christ in ever-increasing revelations. He desires that you expect him to make his presence manifest to you, and more so each passing day.

Believe these promises. Lay hold of these four expectations, and you will see marvelous things in this season of your life.

Dearly Beloved: 49

GRACE AND PEACE TO YOU FROM GOD OUR FATHER.

"Be careful [anxious] for nothing; but in every thing by prayer and supplication with thanksgiving let your requests be made known unto God" (Philippians 4:6).

I believe that prayer mixed with faith is the answer to everything. Paul says here, "in everything" — meaning, "Pray about everything. And give thanks that your requests will be heard and answered." We are told to pray as our first option, not after we have tried everything else in vain. *"Seek ye first the kingdom of God"* (Matthew 6:33).

So many Christians today are being plundered by Satan. Their homes are in turmoil, they are plagued with fear and guilt, they face trouble on all sides. The problems our ministry reads about in letters from Christians are overwhelming.

But to be truthful, so few believers who are facing difficulties turn to the Lord in fervent prayer. Few today have consistent, daily, quality time alone with God in prayer. Too often, despair sets in because they do not go to the secret place to unburden their souls and cry out their sorrows to the Lord. Instead, they tell all of their problems to friends, pastors, counselors — and they neglect the Lord, who waits to have them all alone. We pray as a last resort.

Could God be grieved with this generation the same way he was with Israel? He said of them, *"My people have forgotten me days without number"* (Jeremiah 2:32).

God is pleased when we run to him first, when we make special time to be alone with him, pouring out our innermost feelings and laying our petitions before him. We have no right to say we love the Lord if we don't spend time with him on a regular basis. He will hear your prayers and answer. But he needs you alone so he can speak to you in a quiet moment.

As I go into the Lord's holy presence each day, my most consistent petition is that the Holy Spirit will open God's Word to me so I can be a true oracle of him. I trust him that my messages to the body of Christ will edify, convict and provoke believers to righteousness.

May you make quality time for him, trusting him with your petitions.

Dearly Beloved: **50**

THE LORD BLESS AND KEEP YOU IN HIS LOVE.

Recently, while counseling a Christian man who faced marital, financial and career problems, it dawned on me he was hoping I would say a prayer or give him some kind of supernatural advice to solve his problems. Yet he admitted he himself does not pray. He watches many hours of television, but he doesn't pray or read the Scriptures. I thought to myself, "How many

Christians today face incredibly complex and overwhelming problems, yet never seek God in private prayer?"

May I lovingly ask you some questions? Do you diligently seek the Lord with all your heart and strength regarding your problems and needs? Do you give him quality time in secret prayer, waiting on him? Do you spend at least some meaningful time each day studying his Word? If your answer is no, I would have to honestly say that no one else's prayers will prevail on your behalf. God expects us all to be in agreement in prayer.

His Word promises, *"If you seek the Lord your God, you will find him, if you seek him with all your heart and soul"* (Deuteronomy 4:29).

Until God's people learn to go quickly to him in secret prayer with all their needs and problems, unburdening their souls in his presence, there will be constant disorder and despair. Every time I spend unhurried, quality time with my Lord, I come away refreshed, encouraged and confident God is going to make a way.

If my messages provoke you to get back to praying diligently and in faith, I am convinced you will one day thank me, because you'll see God's blessing and favor on all sides. The Lord deeply loves all who seek his face daily. May he forgive us for neglecting him days on end.

I urge you, begin spending that time with him today. Go to God and pour out your soul in his holy presence.

Dearly Beloved: 51

MAY THE PEACE OF GOD BE UPON YOU.

I was much in prayer about what the Lord would have me say to you. While meditating, the Holy Spirit prompted me to carefully read again Psalms 33 and 34. After reading these two Psalms I knew immediately what the Lord wanted me to do.

I believe that in the following four passages, every single reader of this message will find a special, direct word from the Lord. God is faithful to send his people a word in season, and his Spirit will show you which of the following passages is yours at this very moment in time:

1. *"Behold, the eye of the Lord is upon them that fear him, upon them that hope in his mercy; to deliver their soul from death, and to keep them alive in famine. Our soul waiteth for the Lord: he is our help and our shield"* (Psalm 33:18-20).

2. *"For he spake, and it was done; he commanded, and it stood fast. The Lord bringeth the counsel of the heathen to nought; he maketh the devices of the people of none effect. The counsel of the Lord standeth for ever, the thoughts of his heart to all generations"* (33:9-11).

3. *"I sought the Lord, and he heard me, and delivered me from all my fears. This poor man cried out, and the Lord heard him, and saved him out of all his troubles"* (34: 4, 6).

4. *"The eyes of the Lord are upon the righteous, and his ears are open unto their cry. The righteous cry, and the Lord heareth, and delivereth them out of all their troubles. Many are the afflictions of the righteous: but God delivereth him out of them all"* (34:15, 17, 19).

God bless his precious Word to your heart. He sends his Word to heal.

Dearly Beloved: 52

GOD BLESS YOU MIGHTILY.

As I sat down to write this message, the Holy Spirit prompted me to edify and encourage all readers. I truly believe that the following word is from the Lord, and I pray you will be built up by it in your faith. This is what I believe the Holy Spirit has led me to share with you:

1. The first word is for those who are captive to a besetting sin, lust or habit. You have felt defeated, wicked, helpless. Satan has told you you're evil and that God is turning away from you.

I remind you of what God said to a group of Israelites who were going into Babylonian captivity, a result of their past sins. Even though these Israelites were under discipline for their sins, God called them "good fruit." Then he promised, *"I will set my eyes on you for good... I will build you up, and not pull you down; I will plant you; and not pluck you up. I will give you a heart to know me... I will be your God; you shall return unto me with your whole heart"* (Jeremiah 24:6-7).

All you need is godly sorrow, a desire to be free and a yearning for him. He will not forsake you. He is going to supernaturally change and deliver you!

2. I also have a word for those who feel they have lost direction. You feel confused about a number of issues in your life. You have no one to turn to, and some things appear as if they are out of control. You wonder, deep within your heart, whether you are under some kind of discipline or judgment from God.

Please receive this word from the Holy Spirit: *"O Lord, I know that the way of man is not in himself: it is not in man that walketh to direct his steps. O Lord, correct me, but with judgment (justice); not in anger, lest thou bring me to nothing"* (10:23-24).

79

The Lord will not allow you to be brought down by despair or hopelessness. He will not allow anything in your life to mislead you or confuse you. He will do what is best for you, but never in anger. God is not mad at you. He will direct you, if you will give him your faith, no matter how weak. Trust in his love.

This is the word I know the Holy Spirit has prompted me to send you. May you be encouraged and helped by it.

Dearly Beloved: 53

REJOICE AND BE GLAD IN THE LORD.

Recently I prayed with a dear sister in the Lord who is dying of cancer. She has been in great pain for many weeks. But what a beautiful testimony she is to all who know her. There is no complaining, no sorrow, no questioning of the Lord's greatness and faithfulness. She told me she feels a magnetic pull toward Jesus, and that she is now "there with Christ" more than here on earth. She blessed me with her rejoicing hope and rest in the Lord.

I once heard a very righteous minister say, "I just want to finish my work and get out of here." Some who heard him say this thought he was being unthankful for the gift of life. But the apostle Paul declared virtually the same thing. Paul's constant desire was to be with the Lord. And, beloved, so it is with me. Almost every day I say to Jesus, "I love my family and I thank you for life. But there is nothing here that satisfies — not family, houses, land or comfort. Nothing here can touch my need. This world is only like a mirage. I long to be with you, Lord, in the ultimate reality."

I confess to you, there is one thing I fear more than any other thing in my life: the sin of covetousness. What a damning sin it is: a love for things of this world, a lust for more and better material possessions.

Covetousness has enslaved the hearts of many Christians. People can't seem to get enough, and their debt is piling up. They think our nation's prosperity will never end. Americans have gone mad with acquisitiveness. We are now on a spending spree that has baffled experts.

Jesus warned us to hold lightly to the things of this world. We are to give thanks to him for his blessings, and to give generously to the needs of the poor. But we are never to let anything of this world steal our hearts. We have to be willing to lose it all yet rejoice in his faithfulness.

God does not want us to feel guilty for his blessings upon us, as long as we do not consume them all on ourselves and our family, and we keep it all at arm's length. May the longing of your heart be not for the things of this world, but to be in Jesus' presence — the ultimate reality.

Dearly Beloved: 54

GOD BE PRAISED!

A friend of mine was at his wit's end, despairing, wondering if God had forgotten him in his personal nightmare. He became so desperate one morning that he cried out to God, "Unless you send somebody to give me a word of hope, I cannot make it through the day. I simply cannot go on one more day."

A few hours later, at the point of giving up on life, he went to his mailbox and found a printed message a friend had mailed a few days before. It was a message I released in 1992 entitled, "The Making of a Man of God." It spoke hope and restoration to his sick soul, and he marveled at the timing of the Holy Ghost.

God was right on time with a word of hope especially for him.

Today I am led by God's Spirit to send out just a few words of encouragement to a certain few who will be receiving their own word of hope at just the right time. See if one of the following mini-messages is meant for you:

1. To someone going through a dark night of the soul, feeling God has failed you: voices have confused you. Your Christian friends have deserted you. You feel too defeated to pray. You feel betrayed and even forsaken by God. Your sense of abandonment is frightening. There is a deep sorrow in you. A thought has lingered in your mind that you may have offended God. You have lost all sense of God's love for you. Here is what God has to say to you:

"Can a woman forget her sucking child, that she should have no compassion on the son of her womb? Yea, they may forget, yet I will not forget thee" (Isaiah 49:15).

2. To someone in a marriage crisis: you have been deeply hurt. You want your marriage to be healed and restored but it looks hopeless. You are miserable. You have prayed diligently. You do not want to disobey the Lord, but you see no hope of restoration. I say to you: do not give up on your marriage, no matter how bad things appear.

"I will restore to you the years that the locust hath eaten, the cankerworm, and the caterpillar, and the palmerworm, my great army which I sent among you" (Joel 2:25). *"I have seen his ways, and will heal him: I will lead also, and restore comforts unto him and to his mourners"* (Isaiah 57:18).

3. To somebody who is grieving: something happened to bring down on you a grief, a sadness, a heaviness you can't shake. You love the Lord, but this deep grief is there night and day. You get up with it, you carry it all day, you can't shake it at night. Yet the Lord knows what you are suffering. Here is his word of hope for you:

"I know, O Lord, that thy judgments are right, and that thou in faithfulness hast afflicted me. Let, I pray, thy merciful kindness be for my comfort, according to thy word unto thy servant. Let thy tender mercies come unto me, that I may live: for thy law is my delight" (Psalm 119:75-77).

Dearly Beloved: 55

GRACE AND PEACE TO YOU THROUGH CHRIST OUR LORD.

My office overlooks Broadway and all of Times Square. It is perhaps one the best views of the area, and I am overlooking the square as I write this. Just ahead, I see the building from which the ball is lowered on New Year's Eve, before an anticipated crowd of more than 1 million people.

New Year's Eve at Times Square is a time of drinking, partying and celebrating. And throughout it all, God will not be mentioned or thought of. The multitudes who gather here in a time of unprecedented prosperity will not acknowledge the Lord for any of the blessings we have received. Instead, God will be cursed while pride and flesh are glorified and exalted. Gold is god in this city, as well as throughout the nation.

For the worldly minded, this New Year's Eve represents a time of hope for another year of prosperity and accumulation of goods. Unless there is some kind of economic shaking or a stock market freefall, most Americans will continue their pursuit of the good life and push God even farther from their minds.

Yet, thank God for the holy remnant in America. They are fixing their eyes on Jesus, turning away from fleeting pleasures and the mad pursuit of riches, and looking with ever-increasing yearning for the coming of Christ. They are occupying until he appears.

Beloved, this world is not our home — and our hearts ought to be with our Lord in glory. All the things of this world are going to vanish and fade as dying grass. All the skyscrapers in front of me will one day be dust. As I look out at one of the wealthiest, most glamorous, busiest crossroads of the world, it has no appeal to me — other than as an opportunity to lift up the name of Jesus in the midst of it.

My heart is full of gratitude to God for allowing me to be a part of the witness he has raised up right in the heart of this modern Babylon. May we all give him our thanks for all his blessings, and for his faithfulness to shine the light of Christ in times of spiritual darkness.

Dearly Beloved: 56

MAY THE LORD SHINE ON YOU WITH HIS GRACE AND LOVE.

While praying about what I should share in this message, God's Spirit strongly impressed upon me to talk you about his faithfulness.

"His compassions fail not. They are new every morning: great is thy faithfulness" (Lamentations 3:22-23).

I want to speak to those readers who have failed the Lord. Perhaps you have slipped. Maybe you have become complacent in prayer and Bible reading. Or, maybe you've broken a commandment, sinning against the Lord. You may be under the dominion of a besetting sin. Whatever your situation, you may be overwhelmed with fear, guilt and unbelief. You know God has said he will judge all manner of sin, and now that knowledge has become a burden of fear to you, because you know the Lord is faithful to his Word.

BUT GOD IS ALSO FAITHFUL IN MERCY. In Psalm 89 we find one of the most healing, encouraging words in all of Scripture. God says:

"I have found David my servant...with whom my hand shall be established... I will beat down his foes before his face. My faithfulness and my mercy shall be with him... I will make him my firstborn, higher than the kings of the earth" (89:20-27).

This Psalm is referring to Christ. And it is here the Father establishes a certain covenant with his Son:

"My mercy will I keep for him for evermore, and my covenant shall stand fast with him" (89:28).

Beloved, the same covenant that God made with Christ is made with all of his children.

"His seed [children] also will I make to endure for ever... If his children forsake my law...and keep not my commandments...I will visit their transgression with the rod, and their iniquity with stripes. Nevertheless my lovingkindness will I not utterly take from him, nor suffer my faithfulness to fail. My covenant will I not break, nor alter the thing that is gone out of my mouth" (89:29-34).

Think of it: God has made a covenant never to take his lovingkindness from any of those who are in Christ. He will discipline us with his rod of correction, but he does this in mercy, love and compassion — because whom the Lord loves he chastens. He will be faithful to you in your struggle, enduing you with the power of his Spirit. Christ will not give up on you; he has made a glorious promise to keep you: *"His seed [children] shall endure for ever"* (89:36).

Give thanks to the Lord for his lovingkindness in the morning. Then thank him for his faithfulness every night (see 92:1-2). By faith, receive this healing word.

Dearly Beloved: 57

MAY GOD SHINE UPON YOU WITH ALL SPIRITUAL BLESSINGS.

I am so glad our God sits as King over all floods. Right now our nation is experiencing floods of confusion and disarray. But David says, *"The Lord sitteth upon the flood: yea, the Lord sitteth King for ever. The Lord will give strength unto his people; the Lord will bless his people with peace"* (Psalm 29:10-11).

The prophet Daniel lived in a similar time, saying, *"O Lord, to us belongeth confusion of face, to our kings, to our princes, and to our fathers, because we have sinned against thee... We have not obeyed the voice of the Lord our God, to walk in his laws"* (Daniel 9:8, 10).

The whole world sits in wonderment at the confusion that has fallen upon America. Yet there should be no surprise to those who know the Bible and walk closely with the Lord. We see a pattern throughout the Bible: nations that despised the law of God, flaunting homosexuality and shedding much innocent blood, were cast by the Lord into awful pits of confusion and turmoil.

Yet, in the midst of such judgment, God's people are promised strength and peace. Indeed, there is no confusion in the hearts and minds of praying, trusting believers. Isaiah prophesied that the Lord would give strength and peace to them: *"Thou wilt keep him in perfect peace, whose mind is stayed on thee: because he trusteth in thee"* (Isaiah 26:3).

In these times of upheaval, may you remain in the Lord's perfect peace.

Dearly Beloved: 58

GREETINGS IN THE PRECIOUS NAME OF JESUS.

We live in an age when technology is supposed to provide everything. It should give us all we need without leaving the house. But because of technology, we are now overwhelmed by choices.

When I was a teenager, there were three car companies. Now the choices for car buyers are virtually unlimited. My generation was blown away by the invention of the transistor radio. Today, young people are swamped with choices of dozens of movie screens, many showing filth that we could not have imagined just twenty years ago.

We have been inundated with newly invented things, enticed by new venues of sensuality, promised a longer life span — but we are unable to enjoy what technology has brought. Why?

The current generation is harboring a sense of deprivation. Even our smartest young men and women — Wall Street brokers making hundreds of thousands of dollars a year — feel deprived. They're plagued with a feeling that something is missing, that something is being denied them.

It is called a spiritual vacuum — the syndrome of the empty soul. You see, it doesn't take long to learn that material things are soul-numbing. That is why we see such urgency in the secular world: everybody is racing to reach an unknown goal, an elusive place of peace and fulfillment. One high-flying entrepreneur described this urgency, saying, "Everything new is a pale shadow of what lies ahead. The pace is about to go into hyperactive." Another observer spoke of the soul-numbing effect: "We are becoming a metastasizing organism beyond the reach of any guiding principle."

Thank God for Jesus, our Prince of Peace! Thank the Lord, we who call on his name do not have to be caught up in a mad race for material things. We have found our source of happiness and gladness of heart. Even as I see the world spinning out of control, I can walk these maddening streets of New York City singing, "It is well with my soul."

I pray this is your daily song as well. God bless you with contentment, peace and rest in him.

Dearly Beloved: 59

GOD BE PRAISED!

Are you going through some kind of deep trial? A severe testing? Do you require a miracle to deal with a situation that's beyond your control? Are you desperate for an encouraging word from Jesus right now? If so, the following word is for you.

In Matthew 15, a multitude came to Jesus with various dire needs. Many in that multitude were deaf, blind, maimed, broken or crippled in body. This crowd followed Christ for three days, listening intently to his word, until they *"grew faint"* (15:32). They had seen Jesus' miracles, but still they were faint with bodily hunger.

I am speaking right now to the person who has faithfully sat at the feet of Jesus. You have seen miracles and heard godly teaching. But there is still within you an unmet need, an inner hunger.

Scripture says Jesus had great compassion on the multitude before him. He said, "They have continued with me," meaning, they had not left him. They had endured the hot sun for three days without food, just to *"continue with him"* (15:32). Tell me: are you still continuing with Jesus? If so, you can be assured he has great compassion on you and your physical as well as spiritual needs.

Jesus said firmly, *"I will not send them away fasting, lest they faint away"* (15:32). Do you understand what that means to you and to me? Christ sees your need, and he knows you won't be able to make it unless he performs a miracle. He is still saying, "I will not send you away in need, lest you become a casualty."

With the multitude, it took a miracle on Jesus' part. Their need required immediate action, because another day would have been too late. Even those he had healed would have been falling away due to unmet hunger. So Jesus made them "sit down." There was no panic, no anguish, no one pushing about, saying, "What are we going to do?" They sat — and Jesus was there in their midst.

Beloved, this is what we need to do today as well: *"Be still and know that I am God."*

Jesus is not going to send you on your way when you are hungry or in dire circumstances. You are not to panic or fear. The Lord is still a miracle worker. So, sit down in faith and trust him to provide. Stay close to him, worship him, and do what he has commanded. He has promised to do the impossible, so wait patiently on him. He has an abundant supply and he knows your hurt. Trust him for your miracle of deliverance.

Dearly Beloved: **60**

I am called to edify and build up the body of Christ, and to send forth a clear message that will help conform his people to his image. When we read letters from people telling us my messages help and encourage them, we in turn are encouraged.

While praying over this letter, I felt prompted by the Holy Spirit to send you a further word of encouragement. Are you going through a time of testing and trial at present? Is there suffering of any kind in your life? In your family?

If you will prayerfully read the following Psalms, you will find the Holy Spirit bringing you much encouragement:

• Psalm 46 • Psalm 107 • Psalm 121 (especially verses 7-8).

Be blessed by his Word!

Dearly Beloved: **61**

I GREET YOU IN THE PRECIOUS NAME OF JESUS.

God's Spirit has moved me deeply to send you a note reminding you of the importance of being thankful to the Lord for all his love and blessings to us. Giving him thanks is important, even in the midst of troubles and times of testing.

God had a controversy with Israel because they were not thankful for all his blessings and provision. David understood that God loved to meet every need of his people, but he also knew the Lord wanted their thanksgiving. David wrote, *"Enter into his gates with thanksgiving"* (Psalm 100:4). We are to begin with thanks: *"Offer unto God thanksgiving"* (50:14). *"Let us come before his presence with thanksgiving, and make a joyful noise unto him with psalms"* (95:2).

In recent times of testing, I have found joy and relief in simply going before my Lord with thanksgiving. I tell him I'm overwhelmed and that I'm grateful for all he has done for me in the past. By doing this daily, my soul is lifted above the fray, my joy returns, and I am put at rest.

Have you been thankful to the Lord in recent days? I ask you, aren't there many things for which you can give him thanks? Your salvation. Your health. The comfort and support of the Holy Spirit in your hardest times. His past deliverances.

Paul tells us we should give thanks to God for what we have been taught. His lessons have given us roots with which to withstand the devil in these times. *"Rooted and built up in him, and stablished in the faith, as ye have been taught, abounding therein with thanksgiving"* (Colossians 2:7).

The Lord is calling all of his people to a renewed outpouring of thanks for all he has done for us.

Dearly Beloved: 62

THE LORD BLESS AND KEEP YOU IN ALL YOUR WAYS.

Recently I reread the life story of George Muller who, in the mid-1830s, cared for over 2,000 orphans in England — all by faith in God. Muller was known as the man who got answers to his prayers. Before he died, he had listed in his journals over 50,000 answers to prayer.

When asked how he determined the will of God on any matter, Muller listed the following steps he believed were necessary:

1. "I get my heart into such a state that it has no will of its own in regard to any particular matter."

2. "I do not leave the result to feelings or simple impressions. That can make one open to great delusions."

3. "I seek God's will through, or in connection with, his Word. If you look to the Spirit without the Word, you open yourself to delusion."

4. "I consider providential [God-controlled] circumstances."

5. "I ask God in prayer to reveal his will to me."

6. "I make sure I have a clear conscience before God and man."

7. "Every time I listened to men instead of God, I made serious mistakes."

8. "I act only when I am at peace, after much prayer, waiting on God with faith."

Those who walk by faith, seeking only God's perfect will, are often sorely tested and tried. More and more in my own life, I am finding out how important diligent prayer and Bible reading are. Sadly, not many of God's people pray diligently nowadays. Instead, there is much TV viewing and very little of waiting on God.

When I give myself to prayer, my faith rises. And when I feed on God's Word, my confidence in his power to lead and help me increases. The Lord becomes my banker, my advisor, my attorney, my counselor.

May you find him doing the same for you.

Dearly Beloved: **63**

THE RIVER OF LIFE IS RISING!

Even while death stalks on all sides, the river of spiritual life is rising. And it is healing all it touches.

There is a rising tide of spiritual death in many denominations, as well as in numerous local churches. People are dying spiritually for lack of God's solid Word of truth.

Isn't it ironic that in Russia, China and other countries, people are turning to the Lord with great spiritual hunger and thirst, while here in America abortionists, pornographers and dead denominations are spreading death and mockery of sacred things?

Thank God, his divine purposes will not be hindered one iota. Even now the Spirit of the Lord is moving throughout the world. And here in America, we see pockets of revival and great spiritual hunger.

Are you experiencing more hunger for the Lord and his Word than ever before? That is the work of the Holy Spirit, as he sovereignly raises up a holy remnant. Here in New York City, we are experiencing a flood of God-hungry people who come to church early and leave late. People from all walks of life are becoming conformed to the image of Jesus — rich, poor, homeless, from all nationalities. People are visiting from all over the world, and they too are witnessing "waters to swim in."

The river is rising, and it is bringing spiritual life to all it touches. May it touch you where you are.

Dearly Beloved: 64

THE WORLD IS IN CRISIS — BUT GOD HAS EVERYTHING UNDER CONTROL.

Lately, I have heard many Christians express nagging fears

about the future. Everyone who knows Jesus and knows their Bible understands we are headed for the final wrapping up of all things. It is truly enlightening to discern clearly we are living in the very last of the last days.

But Jesus has a loving warning and command for all his beloved children, and we must take it to heart. He said, *"Ye shall hear of wars and rumors of wars; see that ye be not troubled"* (Matthew 24:6).

The word Jesus uses for "troubled" here means "clamor, wail, be frightened." He's telling us, "In the hour of war and disturbances, do not be afraid. Don't make a fuss over it. See to it your heart is at rest in the Lord."

God said, *"Behold, the nations are as a drop of a bucket, and are counted as the small dust of the balance... All nations are before him as nothing; they are counted to him less than nothing... He shall blow upon them, and they shall wither, and the whirlwind shall take them away as stubble"* (Isaiah 40:15, 17, 24).

Here is reason not to be troubled. God has everything under control!

Dearly Beloved: **65**

HOW FAST THINGS ARE CHANGING!

Things are moving so fast, with events unfolding at such an incredible rate, we have a difficult time keeping up with it all. As a result of this, and all the sudden crises around the globe, there is great fear and anxiety among the unsaved. Jesus warned that such days were coming, when men's hearts would *"fail them with fear because of the things coming upon the earth"* (see Luke 21:26).

I have been prophesying for years about "accelerating

judgments" that will fall upon this nation. Only the spiritually dull and blind can now deny we are seeing last-day judgments upon our nation and the world.

Now is the time to lay hold of TRUST IN THE LORD. God's people are going to have to do more than simply quote Scriptures and sing about living by faith. Times are going to get so troublesome we will need an abiding faith. We are going to have to trust God. Indeed, we'll be forced to prove the Lord is real — not just a dead doctrine, but a living reality who will keep us in the hardest of times.

If you are truly trusting God, you are not afraid. You know God will be faithful to you and yours. You'll be cared for by a heavenly Father who feeds the fowl and the animals, who counts every hair on your head and numbers every sparrow. If the Lord will feed pets and birds in the worst of times, will he not be faithful to feed and clothe his children?

Be encouraged. You are his child — rest in faith daily in his promise to care for you.

Dearly Beloved: 66

PEACE AND LOVE TO YOU FROM OUR BLESSED LORD.

As I was in prayer, the Holy Spirit led me to Psalm 20:1-2:

"The Lord hear thee in the day of trouble; the name of the God of Jacob defend thee; send thee help from the sanctuary, and strengthen thee out of Zion."

THIS WORD IS FOR YOU. Exactly what is the trouble you are facing? Is someone in your family sick or facing a great trial? Is your need financial? Or is the trouble in *you* — some inner struggle with sin or self?

No matter what you're facing, no matter how serious the trouble, the Lord hears the cry of his children *"in the day of their trouble."*

Is there seemingly no one to turn to? *"The name of the God of Jacob defend thee."* The Lord is not your adversary — he is your friend, your great defender. Trust in his name and his power to deliver you.

If all you had was this one promise, it would be enough: *"The Lord send thee help from the sanctuary [the place of prayer and worship]."* In just two verses he has promised to hear you...to defend you...to help you...to strengthen you. How wonderful — believe it!

Dearly Beloved: 67

GRACE AND PEACE BE MULTIPLIED TO YOU.

As I prepared to write this message, the Holy Spirit spoke very clearly to me that I should send you the following encouragement from Psalm 37. I am constantly amazed at how God sends his Word to us just in time, when it is needed most. It is his loving nature to have heard your cry and to have prepared a special word to arrive the very hour you need it. Hear the word of the Lord to you:

1. Do not be upset by evildoers or those who trample you down for their benefit. Their day is coming:

- Psalm 37:1, 2, 7, 8-15, 32-34.

2. Trust in the Lord — delight in him. Turn everything over to him and give rest to your mind and spirit:

- Psalm 37:3-6.

If you will obey this Word, you will be filled with rejoicing and have the desire of your heart. God will bring to pass all he has promised. You will see his righteousness coming forth in you.

3. God knows every step ahead of you. And he is ordering everything pertaining to your life, your family, your needs. So, trust him in everything:

- Psalm 37:23-29.

4. Godly parents do not stay continually angry with their children, just as the Lord is not angry with his children. He wants to be your peace, your strength, and your help in time of trouble:

- Psalm 37:34, 37-40.

The Lord promises to do all these good things for his people in Psalm 37, *"because they trust in him"* (37:40).

Dearly Beloved: 68

GOD GIVES STRENGTH TO THE WEAK.

The Holy Spirit has prompted me to speak to you about thanksgiving. The Hebrew root word for thanksgiving is "adoration." The apostle Paul wrote, *"Giving thanks always for all things unto God and the Father in the name of our Lord Jesus Christ"* (Ephesians 5:20).

The longer I live and the closer I get to the end of my race here on earth, the more I feel the need to adore him through thanking him in all things. *"In every thing give thanks: for this is the will of God in Christ Jesus concerning you"* (1 Thessalonians 5:18).

Giving thanks "in all things" — in *everything*? Yes, in sickness and in health. In good times and in bad. In storms and in sunshine. David said, *"Let us come before his presence with thanksgiving"* *(Psalm 95:2)*. All too often we do not come into the Lord's presence with thanksgiving. Instead, we come to him burdened down with our problems, and fail to give him thanks for keeping us in so many ways. Not one true lover of the Lord can say that he has ever failed.

I ask you, when was the last time you stopped everything to offer thanks to the Lord for what he has done for you? *"O give thanks unto the Lord; call upon his name: make known his deeds among the people. Sing unto him, sing psalms unto him: talk ye of all his wondrous works"* *(Psalm 105:1-2)*.

Dearly Beloved: 69

Paul the apostle wrote: *"God is faithful, by whom ye were called unto the fellowship of his Son Jesus Christ our Lord"* *(1 Corinthians 1:9)*.

This single verse opens us up to a truth that can see us through every storm of life. Here is a simple truth that can keep our hearts at rest when all things around us are shaken. Here is the Word of God that can keep us from the panic and fear that now grip the whole world.

The truth is this: WE LEARN GOD'S FAITHFULNESS BY ANSWERING OUR CALLING TO STAY IN FELLOWSHIP WITH JESUS. *"Called unto the fellowship of his Son Jesus Christ"* *(1:9)*.

We are not called to trust our own intellect. We are not called to trust in flesh, or men, or anything that is of this world. Jesus calls to us, *"Come unto me, all ye that labor and are heavy laden, and I will give you rest"* *(Matthew 11:28)*.

Christ alone is our peace, our confidence and contentment. I have experienced such great contentment when I see by faith my Lord in glory — loving me, calling me into his sweet presence, telling me he is all-sufficient. I don't have to beg or plead or fear. The more I keep looking to Jesus in all things, the more I know he is pleased, because without faith it is impossible to please him.

Sadly, many who truly love Jesus often panic in times of crisis, and they worry and fret. They spend time trying to figure out ways and means to escape or endure their trial. They do not heed his call to "come and dine" with him. I am not talking about spending one hour or so each day in prayer; I'm talking about focusing on him all through the day, "praying without ceasing." This is simple, quiet conversation — just talking to him, becoming more acquainted with him, so that in crisis times we need not rush in consternation to a prayer closet and wail out for help like a stranger.

He hears all cries, loud and soft, and he will always answer us in his faithfulness.

Dearly Beloved: 70

Let me share with you some very healing thoughts about faith and love. I believe God works miracles in answer to the prayer of faith. And I believe every promise in God's Word as is. But, through much suffering and tears, I have discovered something wonderful about the way God works. What you are about to read should help renew your confidence in the Lord and set you free from the bondage of trying to figure out faith.

Here are my conclusions:

1. If you can't give God perfect faith, give him perfect love. "Perfect love casts out all fear." Not perfect *faith*, but perfect *love*. Perfect love is the rest God has for his people. He wants us to rest in his love, trusting that he will always come to our aid as a father to a hurting child in spite of our inadequate faith.

Stop evaluating or grading your faith. And stop trying to figure out faith. The Bible says, *"Now abideth faith, hope, charity, these three; but the greatest of these is charity"* (1 Corinthians 13:13).

If you are going to specialize in anything, specialize in love. The Bible says, "Faith works by love." Without love, all faith is in vain.

2. If God does not answer certain of our prayers, we can be sure he has some great eternal reason for not doing so.

It boils down to this: God has all power and can do anything. Nothing is impossible to him. He has promised to answer every prayer in Christ's name. So we must ask in full assurance of faith, expecting an answer. But should God delay that answer, or choose another path for us, he must have a mighty good reason for it all. And we must believe that whatever God permits in our lives, it will one day all work to our good. *"We know that all things work together for good to them that love God, to them who are the called according to his purpose"* (Romans 8:28).

Our heavenly Father knows exactly where we are going and what we need. He will give us what is best, in proper Holy Ghost timing. *"If ye then, being evil, know how to give good gifts unto your children, how much more shall your Father which is in heaven give good things to them that ask him?"* (Matthew 7:11).

God will not permit you to be overcome by your trials. You may come to what you think of as your breaking point. Yet, if you will not harden your heart but fall into his arms, trusting his everlasting love for you, you will survive and live to tell of his faithfulness.

Dearly Beloved: **71**

THE LORD IS MERCIFUL, KIND AND LONGSUFFERING.

I have a wonderful promise for you today. This special word from the Lord has come to you through his divine providence. Our dear Savior knows what you need to lift your spirit at this time. This is his word for you:

"You have seen my afflictions, you have known the troubles of my soul...you have not given me over into the hand of the enemy" (Psalm 31:7, 8).

"For your name's sake you will lead me and guide me" (31:3).

Beloved, the Lord has his eyes focused on you. He has bottled every tear you've shed in your trials. You are never alone, never out of his sight, and he is touched with the feelings you endure. He will never shut out the cry of your prayer.

Do as David did when he was overwhelmed by circumstances: he encouraged himself in the Lord. Even your closest friends or relatives cannot give you the comfort and direction you need. That is the work of the Holy Spirit. And here is the eternal word you need to be encouraged: THE LORD WILL NEVER TURN YOU OVER TO THE POWER OF SATAN, THE ENEMY (see 31:8).

"Be strong, and let your heart take courage, all you who hope in the Lord" (31:24).

Dearly Beloved: 72

GOD IS STILL ON HIS THRONE.

While in prayer today, the Holy Spirit directed me to Psalm 33. The Spirit whispered to my inner man that there were three nuggets of truth I should share with you in this portion of Scripture. They are as follows:

1. *"Behold, the eye of the Lord is upon them that fear him, upon them that hope in his mercy; to deliver their soul from death, and to keep them alive in famine"* (Psalm 33:18-19). Notice the admonitions: "Fear him." "Hope in his mercy." The word "fear" here does not refer to a slavish, cowering fear. Rather, it speaks of the awesomeness of his great mercy to even the worst of sinners.

Last night I was brought to tears after counseling a Christian brother who had fallen into an old sin. He had consequently fallen into deep depression, insisting that God was punishing him, getting even for his transgression. I pleaded with him to hope in God's mercy — that God was not mad at him, because the Lord in his everlasting mercy never turns away from any of his hurting, repentant children.

God is your keeper. He will keep you from spiritual death. He will keep you alive in times of spiritual famine — if you will fully believe and hope in his mercy.

2. *"Our soul waiteth for the Lord: he is our help and our shield"* (33:20). Verses 13-14 of this Psalm tell us, *"The Lord looketh from heaven; he beholdeth all the sons of men. From the place of his habitation he looketh upon all the inhabitants of the earth."*

As we walk with Jesus, there is not a moment in our lives when his eye strays from us. All things are open to his sight. The problem is, we do not really believe this. In times of deep affliction, we sometimes think he could not be focused on us and that there must be something missing in our theology. Otherwise, we reason, "Why have I hurt so badly for so long? Why is my cry not being heard?"

What do we do when we can't see a way out — when we reach a dead end where there seems to be no answers — and we find ourselves at wit's end? Verse 20 answers us: *"Our soul waiteth for the Lord: he is our help and our shield."* This may sound like unworkable theology, but it is not. In fact, this is the only way out of any and all troubling times: to wait in confidence that God's eye is ever on us. He will come through in his time, which will prove to be the right time.

3. *"Our heart shall rejoice in him, because we have trusted in his holy name. Let thy mercy, O Lord, be upon us, according as we hope in thee"* (33:21-22).

Recently, I proved this passage true. I was called to settle a dispute that seemed humanly impossible to solve. I set my heart to wholly trust God to do the work — to give me words and to send the Holy Spirit to move the hearts of those involved. At first, it seemed like everything would fall apart. But I waited, trusting. When I left, the issues were still unsolved — but still I waited in faith. Later that night, I was called. Those at odds had fallen on their knees and repented, and a great miracle happened before the day ended.

Faith works. And waiting with rejoicing works miracles.

Dearly Beloved: 73

Recently I went to the Lord in prayer very heavyhearted, laden down with many cares. I began to plead my case before him:

"Oh, Lord, I have never been so weary in all my life. I can hardly go on!" Then I began to weep. I was so exhausted, the tears burst out of me. As I lay crying, I thought, "Surely my tears will move the Lord's heart."

The Holy Spirit did come and minister to me — but not in the way I thought he would. I wanted sympathy, encouragement, understanding. And he did give me all of that — but in a way much different from what I expected.

The Lord gently instructed me to go to 2 Corinthians 9:6-11 and said that everything I needed was contained in this passage:

"But this I say, He which soweth sparingly shall reap also sparingly: and he which soweth bountifully shall reap also bountifully. Every man according as he purposeth in his heart, so let him give; not grudgingly, or of necessity: for God loveth a cheerful giver.

"And God is able to make all grace abound toward you; that ye, always having all sufficiency in all things, may abound to every good work: (As it is written, He hath dispersed abroad; he hath given to the poor: his righteousness remaineth for ever. Now he that ministereth seed to the sower both minister bread for your food, and multiply your seed sown, and increase the fruits of your righteousness;) Being enriched in every thing to all bountifulness, which causeth through us thanksgiving to God."

Letters

As I read this passage, and then reread it, I got nothing from it for my situation. Finally, I closed my Bible and prayed: "Lord, I'm confused. I see nothing here to help or encourage me."

Finally, the Spirit spoke forcefully but lovingly to my inner man: "David, this has everything to do with what you're going through. Lately you have been serving me without a bountiful, cheerful spirit. Where is your joy and happiness in your service to me? My Word isn't talking only about giving money to help the poor. It is speaking of ministry to me and to my body.

"I have called you, and I did not send you without help or abundant resources. All that you need is available to you: strength, rest, power, ability, joy and cheer. There is no reason for you to labor with sadness, to be overburdened. You have access to all strength and joy!"

Beloved, rejoice and be glad, no matter what your circumstances. This world needs some godly cheer.

Dearly Beloved: 74

LET US CAST DOWN ALL UNBELIEF.

"He went out from thence, and came into his own country [Nazareth]...and many hearing him were astonished, saying...what wisdom is this which is given unto him, that even such mighty works are wrought by his hands? ...And they were offended at him... And he could do no mighty work, save that he laid his hands upon a few sick folk, and healed them. And he marveled because of their unbelief" (Mark 6:1-3, 5-6).

In the chapter just prior to this, Jesus performed amazing miracles. He cast out a legion of demons from a demoniac. A woman was instantly healed of a hemorrhage that had plagued her for years. A twelve-year-old girl was raised from the dead. When Jesus performed such mighty works, he told those he delivered, *"Thy faith hath made thee whole"* (5:34).

In the next chapter, Jesus came to his hometown, where he met with the worst kind of unbelief. Nazareth was where Jesus had grown up, living his first thirty years. Now he had come back to be among his own people, including his family.

The people of Nazareth had been told of Jesus' great works. They had heard all the amazing stories of the "mighty works done by his hands." Yet, to them, such things happened elsewhere — in other cities, other places, not in Nazareth.

These people were church-going, Bible-loving, sincerely religious. They loved God's Word and said of Jesus, "We know him and his family. He's a good example." But the fact is, these people were spiritually dead. They knew Jesus' reputation as a miracle worker performing mighty deliverances, but they had no faith, no expectancy. In other places, Jesus was met with a hunger, as people pleaded, *"What shall we do, that we might work the works of God?"* (John 6:28). No such question was asked in Nazareth.

This is the tragedy for many Christians today, as well as many churches. They hear of great moves of God elsewhere, with many mighty works being done and multitudes experiencing deliverance. But no one asks, "Why not here? Why not now?"

The Lord chooses not to respond to unbelief. He is grieved whenever his people "limit the Holy One of Israel." Where there is unbelief, there is a dead, dry wilderness. People are left completely without hope. Yet, in truth, there is no such thing as a "dead place." There are only dead Christians who have no faith. Nothing is too hard for God.

Dearly Beloved: **75**

WE HAVE A HIGH PRIEST!

"We have not an high priest which cannot be touched with the feeling of our infirmities; but was in all points tempted like as we are, yet without sin. Let us therefore come boldly unto the throne of grace, that we may obtain mercy, and find grace to help in time of need" (Hebrews 4:15-16).

We are to take everything to Christ. Yet his throne of grace is not a place where we must convince him to help us. He needs no convincing; he is more willing to give than we are to receive.

We have been invited into the throne room of the Potentate of the universe: *"Neither is there any creature that is not manifest in his sight: but all things are naked and opened unto the eyes of him with whom we have to do"* (4:13). Everything is "naked and opened" to the Lord. He knows what you have been through, what you are now going through and facing ahead. And he's not only on your side but waiting for you to come boldly to him.

He is loving, full of mercy, anxious to help you in your time of need. And he is sympathetic, because he himself has experienced all that we are going through, at every point. Simply put, we don't have to explain anything to him: "Jesus, you know what I am going through. I can't put it into words. You've been here before. Help me."

In all of this, we are not to bring into his presence the abomination of unbelief. Instead, we are to "convince ourselves," being "fully persuaded."

"But ye, beloved, building up yourselves on your most holy faith, praying in the Holy Ghost" (Jude 20).

Dear saint, it is time for us to make this our prayer, this very day: "Lord, I have had enough. Do in my life what you are doing in others' and do it here, now, not just elsewhere. When I grow weary in doing your will, I know I can trust you to give me strength, to lift me up. I'm not going to sit around nursing my doubts. I know I have a place to go in my time of need. And I won't measure my spirituality by looking at someone else. I'm leaving all spiritual growth up to you, Lord. I will not listen to the devil's lies any longer. I'm going to build up my faith, in your Word. I know that without faith it is impossible to please you. Amen!"

Dearly Beloved: 76

THE HOLY SPIRIT HAS COME TO LEAD US INTO A LIFE OF PRAYER.

"The Spirit also helpeth our infirmities: for we know not what we should pray for as we ought: but the Spirit itself maketh intercession for us with groanings which cannot be uttered" (Romans 8:26).

Consider what Paul is saying here about the Holy Spirit's role in our prayer life. We get so confused about prayer, making it seem so complicated. If you go into any Christian bookstore, you'll find many books on the subject, with detailed formulas on how to pray.

These multitudes of theories can bring confusion, raising all kinds of questions about prayer: "When does prayer become intercession? Is intercession measured by fervency, or loudness, or the amount of time I spend on my knees? I'm instructed to pray according to God's will, but how do I know his will? And how do I go about praying? Do mental prayers count? What, exactly, do I pray for?"

Such confusion can be so overwhelming, it causes few to pray. There has never been a time when the prayers of God's people are needed more than now. We live in a world gone mad. As global events worsen, conspiring to rob people of peace, societies everywhere are looking for a source of comfort. But they're not finding it in psychotherapy, in dead religion, in causes, even in charity.

The Bible has told us, *"The world does not know Christ. And they will not receive him. But you know him"* (see John 14:17).

At this stage of my life and ministry, one of my greatest concerns has to be that I maintain my prayer life. When I neglect prayer, I grieve the Spirit of God in me. Yes, it is possible for us to grieve the Holy Spirit. Paul writes as much when he says, *"Grieve not the Holy Spirit of God"* (Ephesians 4:30).

Indeed, the Spirit shares God's grief over his people's unbelief and prayerlessness. Consider these few powerful ways the Holy Spirit plays a role in our prayers:

• It is in prayer that the Holy Ghost manifests the presence of Christ in us.

• It is in prayer the Spirit seals God's promises in our hearts.

• It is in prayer the Comforter speaks hope to us.

• It is in prayer the Spirit releases his rivers of comfort, peace and rest in our souls.

Dearly Beloved: 77

YOU ARE NOT ALONE IN THE BATTLE!

Numerous Christians, including some pastors, have told me

they are continually harassed by former sins. They say, "Brother Dave, if you only knew what I once did, how I sinned against such light, you would understand why I'm so down. My sin still hangs over my head, and I battle constant guilt over it. I believe the Lord has forgiven me, that his blood is sufficient to cover my iniquity. But I don't have the peace that comes from that knowledge."

Others tell me, "I believe I'm forgiven, but my mind is continually bombarded with hellish thoughts. It can happen anywhere, even in church, and it makes me feel so unclean. I have a hard time believing I am pure in God's sight."

These believers forget that Satan also tempted Jesus with awful, ugly thoughts during his wilderness testing. Today, the devil sends little foxes into your life to make you think you're hopeless, that God is mad at you. They inject thoughts into your mind meant to destroy your faith in the power of Christ's blood over you.

Dear saint, you are not to listen to those mental invasions. You have to cut them off, crying, "Holy Spirit, I know you're beside me. Help me."

You have to accept that all who take up the cross and fight the good fight of faith are in a constant battle. We are all going to face evil thoughts — thoughts that come because of our past, or because of a sense of rejection, or simply because we live in wicked, sensual times. Yet when we apply Christ's blood to these roots of doubt, it reaches into every cell of our being, including our minds, and thoroughly cleanses us. And that brings freedom and true rejoicing.

You are not alone in your struggle. He has sent you the Holy Spirit, who knows how to deal with the enemy and free you from all bondage. He is the still, small voice that will guide you and empower you through all your battles.

Pray with me: "Holy Spirit, I want to grow in spiritual fruitfulness. I want to be rid of all hypocrisy, and I want gentleness, patience and love. I know you still love me, in spite of my lack of these things. Stand by me, and help me. Amen."

Dearly Beloved: 78

THE RIGHT RESPONSE IN ANY AFFLICTION IS AN INQUIRING HEART.

This is a heart that asks, "Lord, are you saying something to me in this? Have I been blinded to something you want to say to me?" Through the years, I have learned that when afflictions come, I am to run to the Lord with an open heart asking, "What is this all about, Lord? What do you want to show me? I will do whatever you ask of me."

The Holy Spirit never fails to show me. Sometimes he'll say, "This is a snare of Satan, David. Beware." Or, without condemnation, he will reveal an area of compromise, saying, "Obey, and the heavens will open to you. All will become clear."

Our salvation is not in jeopardy. Yet, though we are saved, we still are not fully sanctified. We still have many issues that hinder God's fullness in us, issues of the heart we are blinded to: secret lusts, covetousness, laziness about the things of God. If we're willing to hear him, the Lord will always reveal them to us. Most important of all, if we are enduring the fires of affliction, God will reveal to us his tender, loving mercies and compassion.

When God shows us what is in our hearts — the impatience,

the besetting sin, the "small" but deadening compromises — these things become grievous to us in our time of affliction. It is why David prayed: *"Let, I pray thee, thy merciful kindness be for my comfort, according to thy word unto thy servant. Let thy tender mercies come unto me, that I may live: for thy law is my delight"* (Psalm 119:76-77).

David cried out from his affliction, "Send me your word of comfort, Lord. Show me your tenderness. Show me your loving, everlasting mercy." David was actually claiming a promise God had given him earlier. *"The Lord is gracious, and full of compassion: slow to anger, and of great mercy. The Lord is good to all: and his tender mercies are over all his works"* (145:8-9).

No matter what we are going through, God's mercy is there for us. As David says, his mercy is "over all his works" in all of his people. God is not out to condemn or punish us. Like any loving Father, he tells his children, "Let me love you through this. I want you to know me in the midst of it. I'm using it to show you the depths of my love."

Dearly Beloved: 79

I have a confession to make. The message I'm writing here was born out of deep wounds from friends who turned on me. Sometimes the worst afflictions come from those who are closest to you. Their words and accusations cut the deepest, because they seem to know you the best.

I am thinking of one friend especially whom I had mentored. He came to me making awful accusations, a torrent of hurtful words that wounded me deeply. I went home from our meeting crushed. I fell on my face, pleading with the Lord: "How could my friend say those hurtful things to me? I have never felt so wounded. This is an attack from the enemy. I know in my heart the things he said aren't true."

I forgave my friend for hurting me, and I prayed for him. But something still nagged at me. There was a churning in my spirit that would not stop. I went back to prayer, this time asking, "Lord, are you in this somewhere? Did you allow this? Are you trying to say something to me?"

The Lord answered me with much-needed correction to a particular area in my life. The churning in me over my friend's accusations was actually a wake-up call over an issue that could have destroyed me. It caused me to stop, take a look inside my heart, and ask Jesus to reveal to me anything that was hindering me from moving on in him.

When we humble ourselves in the midst of affliction, God is faithful to give us marvelous revelations of his mercy. He did just that for me. As I received his loving correction, the Holy Spirit whispered to me, "David, go to my Word. Do a search on my mercy, my lovingkindness, my readiness to forgive."

The truth is, whenever God has done a major work in my life, it has been during my darkest hours. I have learned my most lasting life lessons in my times of deepest pain. That is when his mercy came — when I finally stopped trying to figure things out and instead just held on, trusting him to deliver me and work his way in me.

Dearly Beloved: *80*

All of us know what afflictions are. They are those times of trouble and stress that keep us up at night. They can be so painful that we lose sleep because of the anguish and anxiety.

Yet, as painful as afflictions are, God uses them to achieve his purposes in our lives. David writes, *"Many are the afflictions of the righteous" (Psalm 34:19).* Moreover, Scripture makes clear God can use afflictions to heal sinners as well as saints.

I think of Manasseh, the wickedest king in Israel's history. Manasseh turned from the Lord and became a vile, murderous man. Consider all the evil this king did: He raised idols to the pagan god Baal, even in the court of the temple. He built altars for worshiping the sun, moon and stars. He sacrificed his own children, casting them into fiery pits of demonic Baal idols. He scorned the words of righteous prophets and instead sought the counsel of fortune-tellers. He condoned witchcraft, familiar spirits and devil worship. He was a brutal, bloodthirsty tyrant who delighted in murdering innocents. Scripture says Manasseh sinned worse than all the heathen surrounding Israel.

What happened to this wicked king? God sent great affliction upon Manasseh, through the Assyrian army. The dreaded Assyrians invaded Jerusalem and took the people captive, including Manasseh, binding him in chains and wrapping his body in painful thorns. They forced the Israelites into deathly long marches, giving them little to eat or drink. According to historians, these marches were atrocious.

It was during this time of awful affliction that Manasseh began to pray: *"When he was in affliction, he besought the Lord his God, and humbled himself greatly" (2 Chronicles 33:12).* How did God respond to Manasseh's prayer? He heard the king's cries and restored him to his throne. Manasseh then became a fighter for righteousness, tearing down the idols and altars he had built in the land.

The lessons we draw from Manasseh's story are clear. First, how was this man restored? It happened through afflictions. Wicked Manasseh had shut the mouths of the prophets in the land, leaving God one option to get through to him: affliction. That's when the Lord raised up the Assyrians, using them as his rod of correction. A second lesson is, we can never give up on anyone, even the most vile, evil person. God has ways of bringing even the wickedest sinners to himself through affliction.

Dearly Beloved: 81

ALL PRAISE TO GOD FOR HIS CHURCH TRIUMPHANT!

There is a triumphant church rising up even now, coming out of great trials of faith. This last-days church is emerging from fiery furnaces and long days of affliction.

What I see happening is the Holy Spirit at work bringing a people into utter brokenness. He's leading them to a revelation of weakness in their own flesh, in order to show himself strong. I see him bringing his people to the end of themselves, crushing their stubborn wills, until their mindset becomes only, "His will be done." And through it all, they are becoming wholly dependent on the Lord for everything.

Does this describe your situation? Perhaps you've been walking with Jesus for years, and you've never faced a test like the one in front of you right now. Things are coming at you that seem overwhelming, things that only God can do something about. And you realize only he can bring you through.

Right now, Islamics are preparing for a final Jihad, to "take over the world" for Allah. Islamic training camps are rising up worldwide with a message of hate. Yet the Lord has a people in training, a people he's going to use to face down the wrath of this world. He is training and equipping them in his lovingkindness and peace. Our God is a God of love, and he won't use bombs, guns or suicide squads, but an overcoming people who are fearless in the Lord of tender mercies.

All over the world, God's people are experiencing suffering, afflictions and torture more than ever in their lifetime. And of this I am sure: There is a divine, eternal purpose in the intensity of these spiritual and physical battles now being endured in the true body of Christ. *"His tender mercies are over all his works"* (Psalm 145:9).

Our Lord has had a plan all along. God himself came down and took on the form and condition of man, living among sinful men. He endured their hatred, experienced their rejection, faced unthinkable reproach, and through it all he never fought back.

Jesus never established armies of vengeful, hate-filled jihadists. He used no carnal weapons. Instead, he pulled down strongholds by his mighty lovingkindness. Our Lord had but one battle plan: tender, merciful love. Indeed, love drives all of his works on earth. He is the full expression of God's love: *"Blessed be God, even the Father of our Lord Jesus Christ, the Father of mercies, and the God of all comfort"* (2 Corinthians 1:3).

Dearly Beloved: 82

GOD SHOWS US HOW WE CAN LIVE WITHOUT FEAR.

The Apostle John sums it up in one verse: *"Perfect love casteth out fear"* (1 John 4:18). Moreover, the apostle says, *"There is no fear in love... He that feareth is not made perfect in love"* (4:18). In short, if we are living in fear, we can know we are ignorant of perfect love.

Let me point out that John isn't saying, "Perfect love for God casts out all fear." He isn't speaking about unwavering love, or mature love in a Christian, as some interpreters suggest. That isn't where perfect love begins for true believers.

Certainly, we love God, a fact that is beyond doubt. But consider what John says about perfect love earlier in the chapter. *"If we love one another, God dwelleth in us, and his love is perfected in us" (4:12).* According to John, the first consideration of perfect love is unconditional love for our brothers and sisters in Christ.

A Christian can say that he loves God, that he is doing the Lord's will, that he's faithfully performing the work of the kingdom. Such a person may be a worshiper and a teacher of the Word. But if he holds a grudge or speaks against another — if he shuts out anyone in the body of Christ — he walks in darkness, and a spirit of death is on him. All life, all good works, are out of order in this person. Consider what John says of him: *"He that saith he is in the light, and hateth his brother, is in darkness even until now" (2:9).*

If you are interested in living a life without fear, John says, there is a way to get there. Indeed, there is a perfect love that drives out all fear. And here is the first step we all must take: *"Beloved, if God so loved us, we ought also to love one another" (4:11).* The first move is to deal with our relationships in the body of Christ.

According to John, here is where perfect love begins. Loving others is not something we "ought" to do but are commanded to do. We are to love others as Christ loved us. In this is love perfected. Yet, what is meant by love for others? It is more than forgiveness, much more. It is to forgive all transgressions of others toward us. It is to offer them fellowship. It is to esteem them as highly as we do other members of the body.

Dearly Beloved: *83*

I HAVE A WORD FOR YOU ON LIVING AND LOVING AS JESUS DID.

"We have known and believed the love that God hath to us. God is love; and he that dwelleth in love dwelleth in God, and God in him. Herein is our love made perfect, that we may have boldness in the day of judgment: because as he is, so are we in this world" (1 John 4:16-17).

Note the last part of this passage. John tells us we are now living as the Lord lived: forgiving and loving our enemies. There is nothing left in us of revenge, of grudges, of racial prejudice — nothing to condemn us before the Judgment Day. And so now we must know and fully believe the love of God toward us.

"Herein is love, not that we loved God, but that he loved us, and sent his Son to be the propitiation for our sins" (4:10). Do you see what John is saying? Our love for God is a given. Perfect love also means knowing and believing God's love toward us.

Moreover, John says, there must be no fear in this love, no doubting it. Why? If we doubt his love for us, we'll live in torment: *"Fear has torment"* (4:18). Believing in God's love means knowing he is patient with our failures, day in and day out. He hears our every cry, bottles every tear, feels our anguish of heart, and is moved with compassion at our groanings.

This aspect of God's love is vividly illustrated in Exodus, where the Lord sought to reveal his loving nature to his people. He told Moses, "I am going to deliver Israel," and Scripture says:

"They cried, and their cry came up unto God by reason of the bondage. And God heard their groaning" (Exodus 2:23-24). *"The Lord said, I have surely seen the affliction of my people which are in Egypt...for I know their sorrows; and I am come down to deliver them"* (3:7-8).

Do you believe God sees your need and condition, just as he did with Israel? We often glibly say, "Christ is all," and yet when we face a crisis — when one thing after another goes wrong, our prayers seem unanswered, and hope after hope is dashed — we descend into fear. Indeed, we succumb to fear whenever we waver in our trust in the Lord for all things. But the fact is, God never forsakes any child in their time of anguish, even when things seem absolutely hopeless.

Dearly Beloved: 84

I BELIEVE THE LORD HAS GIVEN ME A WORD FOR YOU ON PERFECT LOVE.

When our love is aligned with God's Word — when we embrace his love and care for us, and we love one another unconditionally — only then will we live without fear. We will have boldness on the day of judgment. And we will be able to live in the here-and-now as Christ lived: without fear.

When all fear is gone, we are in perfect love. Listen to these words sung by David: *"Glory and honor are in his presence; strength and gladness are in his place* (1 Chronicles 16:27). The root word for "gladness" in the Old Testament means "jumping for joy" over those enjoying the fullness of perfect love.

Right now, the world is drowning in fear. Humankind trembles over global warming, terrorism, nuclear warfare, a shaky economy, AIDS, mass murders, the rise of Islam, political chaos, wide-spread addiction to drugs, alcohol and porn. I ask you: How can we make any impact for Christ if we are beset with the same spirit of fear that the world has? What kind of hope can we offer — indeed, what kind of gospel do we preach — if it doesn't change us and deliver us from fear?

God brought in the New Covenant to assure his church of his love and full pardon of sin, to bring us into the knowledge of his delight and gladness over us all, that we might know his heart of love for us and live all our days without fear. Consider: *"The ransomed of the Lord shall return, and come to Zion with songs and everlasting joy upon their heads: and they shall obtain joy and gladness, and sorrow and sighing shall flee away"* (Isaiah 35:10).

"The Lord is my light and my salvation; whom shall I fear? The Lord is the strength of my life; of whom shall I be afraid?... Though an host should encamp against me, my heart shall not fear" (Psalm 27:1, 3).

It is long past time for God's people to give everything into his hands. I urge you, stop trying to think your way out of trouble. Instead, rest in the power of God's Word. Let the Lord put gladness in you now, today. Your glad heart will *shock and awe all those who are fearful around you: "Thou shalt become an astonishment, a proverb, and a byword, among all nations whither the Lord shall lead thee"* (Deuteronomy 28:37).

Dearly Beloved: 85

GOD NEVER GIVES UP!

"What man of you, having an hundred sheep, if he lose one of them, doth not leave the ninety and nine in the wilderness,

and go after that which is lost, until he find it?" *(Luke 15:4)*.

Jesus is speaking here of a sheep that had been in the fold. Clearly, this represents a member of Christ's flock, one that's been well fed and led by a loving shepherd. Yet this sheep has gotten lost, so the shepherd has gone out looking for it.

Note what Jesus says about the shepherd here: *"[He goes] after that which is lost, until he find it"* *(15:4)*. God never gives up on anyone who belongs to him and has gone astray. He never allows the downfallen to drift so far they can't be brought back. Instead, God goes out to find that sheep, embraces it and brings it back into the fold.

Simply put, you can go so far into sin that you come to the very brink of hell, and he will still pursue you. David testifies, *"If I make my bed in hell, behold, thou art there"* *(Psalm 139:8)*.

We have all heard the expression "hell on earth." That's what life is like for those who run from God. Their "bed in hell" is an awful, terrible condition. It means to be captivated by sin, drifting further and further from the Lord so that they eventually fall into a lifeless slumber. This slumber is accompanied by a nagging fear that whispers, "You're going deeper and deeper into hell. You may not ever get back to God."

Christ's message to us, however, is, "It doesn't matter what you may have done. You may have made your bed in hell. But you are not too deep in sin for me to reach you and receive you with open arms."

When the shepherd finds the lost, injured sheep, he doesn't take it back to the fold right away. According to the parable, he carries the wounded creature into his house. Then he calls all his friends and neighbors together, exclaiming, *"Rejoice with me; for I have found my sheep which was lost"* *(Luke 15:6)*.

In this last verse, we find the heart of Jesus' message. Christ speaks of the finders rejoicing: *"Likewise joy shall be in heaven over one sinner that repenteth, more than over the ninety and nine just persons, which need no repentance"* (15:7).

Dearly Beloved: 86

YOUR FATHER DELIGHTS IN YOU!

The story of the prodigal, or lost son, is very familiar to most readers, so I won't go into all the details. But I do want to say this about it: it is not primarily about a lost son. Rather, it is about the delight of the father.

To be sure, the parable of the prodigal son is about returning (see Luke 15:11-31). It is also about grace, forgiveness and restoration. But it is not just about the son finally coming home. Read the story again, and you'll note that, significantly, the story doesn't end when he returns.

No, this parable is also about what keeps the son home. What accomplishes this? It is the knowledge that his father delights in him. *"For this my son was dead, and is alive again; he was lost, and is found. And they began to be merry...[with] music and dancing"* (15:24-25).

The prodigal's father never rebuked him, never condemned him, never even spoke about his son running away. Instead, he threw a party for the son and invited all the family's friends and neighbors. This father had been longing for his son to come home, and now it had come to pass.

The prodigal protested at first, telling his dad, "No, no, I'm unworthy." But his father ignored him, calling for a robe to be put on his shoulders, rings on his fingers and shoes on his feet.

Now everything that the father owned was once again made available to the son. And there was great rejoicing, with music, dancing and feasting.

I believe that love brought this young man home. But it was the father's delight that kept him there. You see, the prodigal was kept with the father by the simple act of waking up each day to see that his dad was pleased to have him home. His father delighted at having him present with him. Moreover, everything in that young man's life that had been eaten by the cankerworm was being restored.

I have known many former addicts who are like the prodigal. They can only focus on what was lost years ago because of their habit: a spouse, children, a ministry. They feel the Lord's chastening, and that can be grievous. But Jesus tells them in this parable, "Nothing is lost in my kingdom. You're going to be made stronger through this. You are home now. And my grace will restore you in full."

Dearly Beloved: 87

THERE IS A UNIQUE EXPERIENCE COMMON TO EVERY FOLLOWER OF JESUS.

I'm talking about the tremendous spiritual letdown that follows a mountaintop experience of blessing or victory. We call these experiences "dry spells." They seem like a deep plunge into spiritual darkness, an immersion in great testings, after we have experienced a special touch of God.

We find dry spells plaguing the lives of godly men and women throughout the Bible. It is a common experience, particularly for those who walk closely with the Lord.

The dry spell — the low period in your spirit — is known mostly to those whom God intends to use. Indeed, it is common to everyone he trains to go deeper and further in his ways.

As you look back on your own dry experience, ask yourself: Did such a period follow a renewal of the Spirit in your life? Maybe you experienced a fresh awakening. You went back to earnest prayer, asking the Lord: "Touch me, Jesus. I feel lukewarm. I know my service to you isn't moving forward as it should. I'm hungry to have more of you than I have ever known. And I want zeal to do your works: to pray for the sick, save the lost, bring hope to the hopeless. Renew me, Lord. I want to be used for your kingdom in greater measure."

Because you got serious with God, your prayers began to get answers. You started to hear God's voice clearly. Intimacy with him was wonderful, your zeal was increasing, and you sensed his movement in your life so clearly.

Then one day, you woke up and the heavens seemed as brass. You were cast down and didn't know why. Prayer seemed like agony, and you didn't hear God's voice as you once did. Your feelings seemed dead, your spirit dry and empty. Ever since then, you have had to live only by faith.

Beloved, do not panic! And don't beat yourself up. I know this kind of plunge personally, from the mountaintop to the lowest pit. Peter speaks of it specifically, advising us not to think some strange thing is happening to us: *"Think it not strange concerning the fiery trial which is to try you, as though some strange thing happened unto you. But rejoice, inasmuch as ye are partakers of Christ's sufferings"* (1 Peter 4:12-13). The Lord allows our dry spells because he is after something in our lives.

Dearly Beloved: 88

THE LORD HAS GIVEN ME A SPECIAL WORD FOR YOU ON THE SUBJECT OF "DRY GROUND."

God insists there must be "dry ground" on our way through the Red Sea. He told Israel, *"[You] shall go on dry ground through the midst of the sea"* (Exodus 14:16). Amazingly, God uses this phrase four times, telling his people, "You will go over on dry ground."

We see this phrase again when Israel was poised to enter Canaan. They crossed over Jordan on dry ground on their way into the Promised Land.

Simply put, dry ground is a path. And if you are on it, then you are going somewhere. You are not losing ground or going backward; your dry ground is the Lord's plan, his work in your life, his miracles to perform. You are moving toward a revelation, a new victory in Christ, toward something greater.

Scripture proves this. Note where Pharaoh and his army lost their battle: on God-given dry ground. Dry ground is the exact place where the devil will come after you. He wants to attack you when you are at your weakest. Yet it is on this same dry ground that the Lord removes the "chariot wheels" from Satan's principalities and powers: *"The waters returned, and covered the chariots, and the horsemen, and all the host of Pharaoh that came into the sea after them; there remained not so much as one of them"* (14:28).

God is telling us, in essence: "I want you to learn to move on in faith — not according to a vision or a voice, but when you are in the midst of a dry spell. I want you to be confident that when you can't hear my voice or see ahead — when you are on dry ground — I am leading you somewhere."

Moreover, the Lord promises that out of our dry places, new life will spring up. He will turn our dry ground into springs of fresh water: *"When the poor and needy seek water, and there is none, and their tongue faileth for thirst, I the Lord will hear them, I the Lord will not forsake them. I will open rivers in high places, and fountains in the midst of the valleys: I will make the wilderness a pool of water, and the dry land springs of water"* (Isaiah 41:17-18).

Dear saint, are you dry? God is telling you, "Soon you will see a harvest. Where there once was dry ground, life will spring up at your feet. And I have created it! Stand still, and see what I will do for you on dry ground."

Dearly Beloved: 89

THE HOLY SPIRIT IS HERE.

At Times Square Church, we sing a hand-clapping song that goes this way:

Send him on down, Lord, send him on down.
Lord, let the Holy Ghost come on down.
We need him, Lord, send him on down.

The truth is, the Holy Spirit is already here. He came down from heaven at Pentecost. And he never left!

Jesus promised, *" I will pray the Father, and he shall give you another Comforter, that he may abide with you forever, even the Spirit of truth; whom the world cannot receive, because it seeth him not, neither knoweth him: but ye know him; for he dwelleth with you, and shall be in you"* (John 14:16-17).

Consider a phrase Jesus uses here: "But you know him." Recently, as I read those words for my study in preparing this message, I could not shake them off. I realized I really don't know much about the Holy Spirit.

The church talks a lot about the Spirit. We teach a doctrine of the Holy Spirit. We talk about being filled with the Spirit, living and walking in the Spirit, having the gifts of the Spirit, receiving the comfort of the Spirit.

Yet it is possible to know all the doctrines of the Holy Spirit and still not know him. If I were to ask you, "Have you received the Holy Spirit?" how would you answer?

Some might say, "Yes, I received the Spirit when Jesus saved me. It was the Holy Spirit that brought me into Christ's kingdom." Others would answer, "Yes, I have received the Spirit, because I spoke with tongues when he came into my life. I pray in the Spirit, and tongues are an evidence that I have received him."

However, to receive the Spirit is more than a one-time experience. The word "receive" means "lay hold of that which is given." In short, receiving is to desire an expanding capacity for greater knowledge of who the Spirit is and what his ministry is about. In fact, the Holy Spirit is not received by someone until he is allowed to take full control of that person's temple.

Paul asked the Galatians, "How did you receive the Spirit? Did you not receive him by faith?" He then declares, "You stated that what you know of the Spirit you received by faith. So, has there been a continued 'ministry of the Spirit' to you by faith? Are you exercising faith to go deeper in the Spirit?"

Dearly Beloved: **90**

THE COMFORTER HAS COME!

Jesus calls the Holy Spirit "the Comforter." It is one thing to know the Holy Spirit as our Comforter. But we must also know *how* he comforts us, so we can distinguish what comfort is of flesh and what is from the Spirit.

Consider the brother or sister who is overcome with loneliness. This person prays for the comfort of the Holy Spirit and expects that comfort to come as a feeling. He imagines it as a kind of sudden breath from heaven, like a spiritual sedative to his soul.

But the next morning, the feeling of peace is gone. As a result, he starts to believe the Holy Ghost has refused his request. No, never! The Holy Spirit doesn't comfort us by manipulating our feelings. His way of comforting is vastly different and is outlined clearly in Scripture. No matter what the problem, trial or need, his ministry of comfort is accomplished by bringing truth: *"[The] comforter...even the Spirit of truth"* (John 14:16-17).

The fact is, our comfort springs from what we know, not what we feel. Only truth overrules feelings. And the comforting ministry of the Holy Spirit begins with this foundational truth: *God is not mad at you. He loves you.*

"Hope maketh not ashamed; because the love of God is shed abroad in our hearts by the Holy Ghost which is given unto us" (Romans 5:5). The Greek meaning here is even stronger than the translation suggests. It says that the love of God is caused to "gush forth" in our hearts by the Holy Spirit.

An unbearable burden may be caused by fear, shame, sorrow, afflictions, temptations, discouragement. Yet no matter what the cause, comfort is needed.

Now, suddenly, a voice is heard echoing through every corridor of the soul. It is the voice of the Holy Spirit, declaring to the soul, "Nothing can separate you from the love of God."

This truth — once you believe it — quickly becomes a gusher of living water, sweeping away every stumbling block. *"The Comforter, which is the Holy Ghost, whom the Father will send in my name, he shall teach you all things, and bring all things to your remembrance, whatsoever I have said unto you"* (John 14:26).

The Holy Spirit plays a central part in our sonship to the Father. The Spirit is our teacher in our everyday walk with Christ, and we are his students. And he teaches us that we are adopted. We are God's family, his sons and daughters.

Dearly Beloved: 91

I HAVE A WORD OF ENCOURAGEMENT FOR YOU ABOUT THE WAR WE ARE IN.

The Holy Spirit has come to wage war against the lusts and enticements of our flesh. *"The flesh lusteth against the Spirit, and the Spirit against the flesh: and these are contrary the one to the other: so that ye cannot do the things that ye would"* (Galatians 5:17).

An inner war still rages within us. Every Christian can say, "I know God loves me. I know him as my Father, and I know I am his child. I know I am made righteous in God's eyes, and I have access to my Lord. But there is still a war going on inside of me. I still fight against fleshly thoughts, against awful temptations. And this war never seems to end."

Beloved, this war is a reality for every Christian. We think thoughts that are unworthy of Christ. We look at things we ought not to, we are tempted by things we shouldn't be tempted by, we listen to talk we shouldn't give ear to. And it all makes us feel unworthy and unclean.

These battles can be so intense and so ongoing, at times we feel we're losing the war. Even the apostle Paul felt this way, crying out in anguish, *"Who shall deliver me from the body of this death?"* (Romans 7:24).

Yet in response to our cries, the Holy Spirit comes with truth that brings comfort: *"There hath no temptation taken you but such as is common to man: but God is faithful, who will not suffer you to be tempted above that ye are able; but will with the temptation also make a way to escape, that ye may be able to bear it"* (1 Corinthians 10:13).

In short, Paul says, you are fighting the same warfare that is being experienced by godly saints all over the world. Your trial is not something peculiar or specific to you. The apostle Peter assures us as well: *"Beloved, think it not strange concerning the fiery trial which is to try you, as though some strange thing happened unto you"* (1 Peter 4:12).

The reason your flesh has risen up — the reason Satan has enflamed you — is because you have invited the Spirit to move in and take control. But the Holy Spirit is more than conqueror over your flesh. That's why Paul gives us these words: *"[God] will with the temptation also make a way to escape, that ye may be able to bear it"* (1 Corinthians 10:13).

Dearly Beloved: 92

There is something I believe grieves God's heart. It is when those who confess Christ and have been forgiven continue to live in fear and unbelief. I speak of those who have known conviction for their sin. They've known godly sorrow over their trespasses, and they have testified that they've been forgiven. But they haven't yet entered the rest and joy that come from forgiveness through repentance.

The burden of sin — the memories and hauntings of past sins — must not be carried beyond the Cross.

All mourning over past sins, all self-imposed humiliation, must be cast into the cleansing fountain of Christ's blood. Ultimately, there comes a time when all who follow Jesus must hear him say, *"Come unto me, all ye that labor and are heavy laden, and I will give you rest"* (Matthew 11:28).

The Lord calls out to all who have confessed, repented and believed yet who can't rejoice because they still carry a heavy burden of guilt and condemnation. All of these he calls to come to him and give him their heavy burden, and he will give them gladness of heart.

When we do this, the Holy Spirit comes to stand beside us. Jesus called the Spirit "the Comforter," a name that means "one who comes and stands by." In short, from that point on we no longer walk alone, in our own efforts, but in cooperation with the Holy Spirit.

This is because of the New Covenant that God made with believers in these last days. According to Hebrews, this covenant went into effect the moment Jesus drew his last breath: *"A testament [or covenant] is of force after men are dead; otherwise it is of no strength at all while the testator liveth"* (Hebrews 9:17).

What is the gift of inheritance that Jesus has left us through his testament? It is this promise: *"I will be merciful to their unrighteousness, and their sins and their iniquities will I remember no more"* (8:12).

Yet we are given more than forgiveness through this New Covenant. God gives us a further word of deliverance, saying he is *"working in you that which is well-pleasing in his sight, through Jesus Christ; to whom be glory for ever and ever"* (13:21).

Dearly Beloved: 93

MAY THE JOY OF JESUS FLOOD YOUR SOUL.

Economic conditions keep growing worse. News reports are fueling the panic, and even people of seasoned faith experience pangs of anxiety. Many of America's most powerful banks have been taken over by the government, and we saw pictures of hundreds lining up trying to get their money out. But where do you put it then? There are no more safe havens.

Truly God's Word is fast being fulfilled: all is being shaken, exactly as we were warned. NOW IT IS PROVING TIME!

We who know God as Father — we who have boasted all these years that he is our strength, our provider, our hiding place, our strong tower, our protector, our deliverer — must now show the world that the God we serve will do all he promised.

We will be facing times that test us beyond our ability to endure. But that is why God sent the Holy Spirit to abide in us. He is truly the Comforter, our guide, for times like these.

If we find a place alone with the Lord daily — pouring out our hearts to him, putting our fears on him, asking the Holy Spirit to guide us each day — we will not live in panic. Fear is a tormenter. And Jesus has told us, "Let not your heart be troubled, neither let it be afraid." To do this, we must make a new commitment when we rise to face each day. This is a commitment of everything — every situation, every relationship — into the hands of the Lord. We are going to find our God has everything under control. Indeed, his angels are on assignment even now to keep us from falling.

Dearly Beloved: **94**

GOD'S MERCIES ENDURE FOREVER.

I wish to give God praise and thanks for his goodness and mercy.

First of all, I want to thank the Lord for giving me the opportunity to conduct ministers' conferences around the world. In recent years, we have had conferences in over 50 nations.

I thank God for the continued blessing and moving of the Holy Spirit at Times Square Church here in New York City. Growing numbers are coming to Christ and the presence of the Lord is awesome. To God be the glory!

I thank God for his blessing upon all our missions outreaches. We are rejoicing that the Lord has enabled us to support so many orphanages around the world with year-round support. For a good number of these orphanages, we are their major support.

We have not done much publicity of our numerous ministries to the needy worldwide. The following is a partial list of what we have provided:

Fifty roofs for poor churches in Kenya. Feeding programs in Kenya, Latin America, the Far East, Africa and South America. Generous funds for earthquake victims in Peru and elsewhere. Funds for widows and homeless children. Small motorcycles for poor pastors who have no transportation. Support for missionaries in various nations. Funds for drug and alcohol rehab centers, where addicts and alcoholics are being saved and many called to preach. Construction of small houses in slums and in flood and quake areas.

All these and more are supported by faith alone. We have no fund raisers, no public relations director. We pray in the funds needed. I want to praise the Lord for meeting all our needs for the past 55 years of ministry to the poor and needy. God is faithful!

Dearly Beloved: **95**

SCRIPTURES TO LIVE BY IN PERILOUS TIMES.

I am led of the Holy Spirit to give you some powerful promises from God's Word, to keep and protect you and your family in chaotic times.

• Psalm 17:7-8: *"Show thy marvelous lovingkindness, O thou that savest by thy right hand them which put their trust in thee from those that rise up against them. Keep me as the apple of the eye, hide me under the shadow of thy wings."*

• Psalm 27:5: *"In the time of trouble he shall hide me in his pavilion: in the secret of his tabernacle shall he hide me; he shall set me up upon a rock."*

• Psalm 31:7: *"I will be glad and rejoice in thy mercy: for thou hast considered my trouble; thou hast known my soul in adversities."*

• Psalm 32:6-8: *"For this shall every one that is godly pray unto thee in a time when thou mayest be found: surely in the floods of great waters they shall not come nigh unto him. Thou art my hiding place; thou shalt preserve me from trouble; thou shalt compass me about with songs of deliverance. I will* instruct thee and teach thee in the way which thou shalt go: I will guide thee with mine eye."

• Psalm 34:17: *"The righteous cry, and the Lord heareth, and delivereth them out of all their troubles."*

• Psalm 34:22: *"The Lord redeemeth the soul of his servants: and none of them that trust in him shall be desolate."*

• Psalm 37:3: *"Trust in the Lord, and do good; so shalt thou dwell in the land, and verily thou shalt be fed."*

• Psalm 37:25: *"I have been young, and now am old; yet have I not seen the righteous forsaken, nor his seed begging bread."*

• Psalm 56:3-4: *"What time I am afraid, I will trust in thee. In God I will praise his word, in God I have put my trust; I will not fear what flesh can do unto me."*

• Psalm 56:11: *"In God have I put my trust: I will not be afraid what man can do unto me."*

• Psalm 66:20: *"Blessed be God, which hath not turned away my prayer, nor his mercy from me."*

• Psalm 72:12-13: *"He shall deliver the needy when he crieth; the poor also, and him that hath no helper. He shall spare the poor and needy, and shall save the souls of the needy."*

A closing testimony: I want to thank God for supplying the funds to keep supporting all our commitments to orphans, feeding ministries and missionary outreaches around the world. God is so faithful. We trust him for all provisions in the days ahead.

Part 2
Dearly Beloved Messages

Dry Spells

There is a unique experience common to every follower of Jesus. I'm talking about the tremendous spiritual letdown that follows a mountaintop experience of blessing or victory. We call these experiences "dry spells." They seem like a deep plunge into spiritual darkness, an immersion in great testings, after we have experienced a special touch of God.

We find dry spells plaguing the lives of godly men and women throughout the Bible. It is a common experience, particularly for those who walk closely with the Lord.

Consider Elijah.

This bold prophet led an amazing life of faith. In a single day, God manifested his power in Elijah in incredible ways. At Mount Carmel, the prophet called down fire from heaven that consumed his sacrifice along with twelve barrels of water. Elijah then wiped out 400 priests of Baal. As the people beheld this amazing scene, they fell down on their faces in worship.

We also see Elijah doing other incredible works. He prayed down rain to end a drought and he outran King Ahab's chariot over many miles. Talk about glorious manifestations of God's power. These were incredible victories, marvelous answers to the prayers of a godly man. Elijah was experiencing supernatural strength, the very power of the Holy Spirit. He was bursting with zeal and faith, walking on an elevated spiritual plane.

So, what followed for Elijah? In the very hour of his blessing and revelation, this mighty prophet plunged deep into despair. Ahab's wife, Queen Jezebel, had threatened to kill him – and suddenly, in a day's time, Elijah descended from glorious victory to utter despair. A dryness overcame him, and his spirit got so low he wanted to die.

Elijah ended up running from God in fear. He couldn't shake his despair, so he hid out in a cave, crying, "Lord, I have failed in my mission. What purpose is there to my life?" He was experiencing a dry spell.

Consider David.

God told this man, "I am going to establish your kingdom as everlasting." *"Thine house and thy kingdom shall be established forever before thee"* (2 Samuel 7:16).

When the Lord spoke this word to his servant, he was referring to David's seed or lineage. Of course, God was speaking also of the Messiah to come. No man could have been blessed more than David was by this promise.

After the incredible revelation, David went from one mountaintop experience to another. Scripture repeatedly says of his life, *"And after this, David…"*, recording victory upon victory, blessing upon blessing. With awesome anointing, David subdued enemy after enemy and recovered Israel's borders, strengthening the kingdom. He was enjoying blessings on all sides, and as he worshipped in the temple he asked the Lord, "Who am I to be so blessed by you?"

What followed for this great servant of God? Here he was at the height of his most victorious, blessed time: so close to the Lord, hearing God speak in such clarity, being fruitful, seeing wonderful promises fulfilled. Scripture tells us it was at the very peak of this experience that David fell into a pit of awful temptation.

What followed was the most vicious dry spell David would ever experience. We have read his confession about the spiritual drought that came after his fall. David cried, "My soul is cast down, my bones ache, all joy has departed. I was so blessed, but now I am lonely and down. I can't understand it. Oh, God, where are you?"

Consider the apostle Peter.

Jesus had just been crucified and buried when Peter and the disciples decided to meet. They convened behind a locked door, fearing for their lives, when they heard these exciting words: "He is alive!" Suddenly, Jesus walked through the locked door in his resurrected body. He told the disciples gathered there, *"Fear not. It is I, your Lord."*

Now, if you had been in the room that day, wouldn't you say this was the most incredible sight you could ever witness? Think of it: with your very own eyes you see the risen Christ, shortly before he ascends to his heavenly throne. You are allowed to touch him, embrace him, sit down to eat with him.

Before he leaves, Jesus commands you to go into all the world, preaching and baptizing, casting out devils and healing the sick. And he promises his presence will never leave you: "I will go with you to the ends of the world."

I tell you, any believer in that room would consider this the greatest revelation, the most glorious moment, anyone could ever experience on earth. Anyone in that room would think, "I'm going to have a miracle ministry. Jesus said so. He's going to use me as I never could have imagined."

Tell me, wouldn't that experience build up in you a reservoir of faith? Wouldn't you be convinced you could never doubt again?

Yet, what followed this greatest of all spiritual highs? *"Peter saith unto them, I go a-fishing" (John 21:3).* In effect, Peter abandoned his call to ministry and returned to his former life as a fisherman. And six of the disciples followed Peter to the lake. Why? What had happened to the great ministry that Jesus summoned them all to?

These men had fallen into deep sorrow. It was something Jesus had forewarned them about: *"In a little while, and ye shall not see me...and ye shall be sorrowful" (16:19-20).* Christ knew these devoted followers would experience a very low period. They were going to be overwhelmed by his physical absence in their lives; there would be no more face-to-face communion with him. Though he had promised he would be with them, it seemed he was leaving them to make it on their own.

T. Austin-Sparks, a godly minister who lived a century ago, testified, "There are times the Lord lets us feel that we are left alone, when he seems to close the heavens and there is no to-and-fro communication. Everything we had looked for and expected seems to have come to an end, to have broken down. All seems to be in ruins" (my close paraphrase).

Let me share with you a personal experience of a dry spell.

In 1974, I was at a convention in Dallas where I spoke on "The Sufferings of Christ." In the middle of my message, the Holy Spirit came upon me and I began to exalt the Lord. As I raised my hands to heaven, I was moved to speak only these three words: "Glory, honor, praise."

In an instant, I was swept up in a river of praise to the Lord. I was caught up in the Spirit, as though I were being lifted out of the auditorium. Suddenly, my praises were joined with those of angels and heavenly hosts. I felt as if I were but one voice in heaven's choir.

I collapsed on the podium while the audience sat still. There was light all around me, and it grew increasingly brighter. I seemed to be in some kind of heavenly atmosphere. In that moment, the presence of Jesus was all in all to me. I had no desire to meet Moses or Abraham or even loved ones who had gone on before. I had no concern for streets of gold or mansions. The question "Will we know each other in heaven?" didn't even apply. None of those things mattered. The glory of God's presence was completely overpowering to me. I began to realize how little we know about the glory of Christ.

I knew that what I was experiencing was not a result of my holiness. On the contrary, I had failed the Lord often. The fact is, I was in a realm of high praises to him. I realize now this was God's answer to my soul's cry, my hunger for him, my prayers for a greater revelation of Christ. I was being given a vision of how our praises here on earth blend in with the praises of heaven's hosts.

Finally, I awoke from the experience and sat up. My wife, Gwen, who was on the podium with me, was relieved. It was a while before I could speak.

In the wake of that experience, I thought, "I have had a glimpse of his glory! This is the greatest single revelation in my life. My flesh has been defeated by this experience. I'll never again go down into a valley of despair. From now on, I will pray like Elijah. Revelation after revelation is going to flow. I will never do anything to cause me to lose this glow."

Less than a week after that, I entered into the driest period of my life. Over the next six weeks, I seemed to go from the heavenlies to agonizing emptiness. I had thought tremendous growth would follow my experience, that my hunger for truth would grow and I would have ever-increasing joy and peace. Instead, the heavens seemed shut to me.

I know God was not literally hiding from me, because he promises never to leave us or forsake us. I sought the counsel of several pastors, one of whom told me my dry spell was God's way of showing me that emotional experiences have no value. I knew that wasn't the case for me. Nobody could take away the deep experience of high praises the Lord had given to me.

Over time, I became convinced that I was sharing an experience so many other believers have known: *spiritual dryness and testing after fresh revelation.*

There were times during my ministry when I was privileged to partner with great men of God, such as Leonard Ravenhill, who wrote *Why Revival Tarries.* At times these men would share with me their deep experiences in their dry spells. As they spoke, inside I recoiled. In my youthful zeal I thought, "This shouldn't be. I know this man is a giant in the faith. Lord, where is he falling short, that he has come to such a wilderness?"

I did not understand the deep, awesome work of the Spirit that God does on dry ground.

Have you experienced dry spells like these?

I have offered examples of the highs and lows of major figures from the Bible. I have described one of my own dry experiences and mentioned those of godly men in my life. I ask you, what experience have you had with extreme lows after spiritual highs?

Both in Scripture and in my experience, the dry spell — that low period in your spirit — is well known to those whom God intends to use. Indeed, it is common to everyone the Lord trains to go deeper and further in his ways.

As you look back on your own dry experience, ask yourself: did such a period follow a renewal of the Spirit in your life? Maybe you experienced a fresh awakening. You went back to earnest prayer, asking the Lord: "Touch me, Jesus. I feel lukewarm. I know my service to you isn't moving forward as it should. I'm hungry to have more of you than I have ever known. And I want zeal to do your works: to pray for the sick, save the lost, bring hope to the hopeless. Renew me, Lord. I want to be used for your kingdom in greater measure."

Because you got serious with God, your prayers began to get answers. You started to hear God's voice clearly. Intimacy with him was wonderful, your zeal was increasing, and you sensed his movement in your life so clearly.

Then one day, you woke up and the heavens seemed as brass. You were cast down and didn't know why. Prayer seemed like agony, and you didn't hear God's voice as you once did. Your feelings seemed dead, your spirit dry and empty. Ever since then, you have had to live only by faith.

Beloved, do not panic! And don't beat yourself up. I know this kind of plunge personally, from the mountaintop to the lowest pit. Peter speaks of it specifically, advising us not to think some strange thing is happening to us: *"Think it not strange concerning the fiery trial which is to try you, as though some strange thing happened unto you. But rejoice, inasmuch as ye are partakers of Christ's sufferings"* (1 Peter 4:12-13).

When I woke to dryness one day, after that great mountaintop experience in Dallas, I became introspective. I tried to retrace my steps to see where I might have possibly derailed. As I examined my heart, I ended up blaming myself for having a hard head, thinking I was unable to "get" the deep things of God.

The truth is, if you are on dry ground, you are on your way to greater miracles.

God insists there must be "dry ground" on our way through the Red Sea. He told Israel, *"(You) shall* go on dry ground *through the midst of the sea"* (Exodus 14:16, my emphasis). Amazingly, God uses this phrase four times, telling his people, "You will *go over on dry ground."*

We see this phrase again when Israel was poised to enter Canaan. They crossed over Jordan *on dry ground*, on their way into the Promised Land.

Simply put, dry ground is a *path*. And if you're on it, you are going somewhere. You're not losing ground or going backward; your dry ground is the Lord's plan, his work in your life, his miracles to perform. You are moving toward a revelation, a new victory in Christ, toward something greater.

Scripture proves this. Note where Pharaoh and his army lost their battle: *on God-given dry ground.* Dry ground is the exact place where the devil will come after you. He wants to attack you when you're at your weakest. Yet it is on this same dry ground that the Lord removes the "chariot wheels" from Satan's principalities and powers:

"The waters returned, and covered the chariots, and the horsemen, and all the host of Pharaoh that came into the sea after them; there remained not so much as one of them" (Exodus 14:28). Simply put, our enemy is defeated *on dry ground.*

God is telling us, in essence: "I want you to learn to move on in faith – not according to a vision or a voice, but when you're in the midst of a dry spell. I want you to be confident that when you can't hear my voice or see ahead — when you are *on dry ground* — I am leading you somewhere."

Moreover, the Lord promises that out of our dry places, new life will spring up. He will turn our dry ground into springs of fresh water:

"When the poor and needy seek water, and there is none, and their tongue faileth for thirst, I the Lord will hear them, I the God of Israel will not forsake them. I will open rivers in high places, and fountains in the midst of the valleys: I will make the wilderness a pool of water, and the dry land springs of water.

"I will plant in the wilderness the cedar, the shittah tree, and the myrtle, and the oil tree; I will set in the desert the fir tree, and the pine, and the box tree together: that they may see, and know, and consider, and understand together, that the hand of the Lord hath done this, and the Holy One of Israel hath created it" (Isaiah 41:17-20, my emphasis).

Dear saint, are you dry? God is telling you, "Soon you will see a harvest. Where there once was dry ground, life will spring up at your feet. And I have created it! Stand still, and see what I will do for you *on dry ground*."

The Most Important Issue of This Hour

Christ asked, *"When the Son of man cometh, shall he find faith on the earth?" (Luke 18:8)*. When the Lord asked this question, he was raising what I believe is the most crucial question of our time or any time. It is a question especially important for Christians who are enduring suffering or deep afflictions.

Let me give a context for Jesus' question here. He had just told the story of a persistent woman who came to a judge asking him for justice in her case. Jesus points to this woman as an example of the kind of persistent, enduring faith he is looking for: the kind that calls upon God in times of trial and trusts him to fulfill his promises.

Christ knew such enduring faith is the only kind able to sustain his followers in their most turbulent hour of testing. In other words, when their prayers are not being answered — when the deadlines for their requests are not met — will they continue to cling to the Lord? Or will they fall into unbelief?

"He hath no root in himself, but dureth for a while: for when tribulation or persecution ariseth because of the word, by and by he is offended" *(Matthew 13:21, my emphasis)*. Too often, when afflictions start showing up in believers' lives, they become "offended," as Jesus says.

You've probably heard such "offense" expressed by Christians who have faced dire afflictions. They have read God's Word, they have claimed certain promises, they have prayed earnestly, but still their trial continues. And over time, because they haven't seen an answer to their prayers, they become offended by the Word they've been clinging to.

At some point, a seed of unbelief is planted in their heart. And soon they begin to question God's faithfulness. They can't shake the nagging thought that the Lord has failed to keep his promises to them.

You probably know such believers. Their trust in the Lord has been well known. Whenever you talked with them, their conversation was full of faith, and they testified of God's trustworthiness. But now you've begun to hear little doubts in their speech. Instead of faith, you hear a certain questioning, remarks that betray an inner unbelief.

Does what I describe here strike a chord in your soul?

I must ask you: have you allowed seeds of unbelief in your heart? Do you have serious questions regarding God's faithfulness? Instead of worshiping him, do you now doubt him, asking, "Lord, why haven't you intervened for me? Why have you allowed such turmoil in my marriage, such confusion in my family? You have put on me more than I'm able to bear."

The apostle Paul exhorted Timothy, *"Endure hardness, as a good soldier of Jesus Christ"* (*2 Timothy 2:3*). The Greek word for "hardness" here indicates suffering, difficult afflictions. Paul says of such things, "Endure them, son! You are a soldier in the Lord's army. You've been trained to undergo hardship in spiritual battle."

We see this truth reflected in the Old Testament as well. We are told, *"The eyes of the Lord run to and fro throughout the whole earth, to show himself strong in the behalf of them whose heart is perfect towards him"* (*2 Chronicles 16:9*).

The Hebrew word for "perfect" in this verse means "wholly given to him in trust." In short, whenever the Lord finds such a servant, he says of that person, "This beloved one is holding fast to his faith and confidence in me. Therefore, I will show myself strong to him. He's going to know my power, to see my strong arm revealed on his behalf."

This verse was first spoken to King Asa, ruler of Judah.

The searching eyes of the Lord had come upon King Asa, who was loved because he "did what was right before God's eyes." By every measure, Asa was a righteous man who trusted the Lord. He walked in faith, wholly dependent on God, and his actions proved it. Asa wiped out idolatry in the land, tearing down all false gods. He abolished witchcraft, sodomy and prostitution. And he built up the cities, with strong towers, high walls and secure gates.

Under this faithful king's rule, the nation of Judah prospered and was blessed. And Asa reminded the people that all their blessings had come to them *"because we have sought the Lord our God, we have sought him, and he hath given us rest on every side. So they built and prospered"* (2 Chronicles 14:7).

But suddenly one day that peaceful environment changed. A messenger brought to Asa a frightful report: a million-man army was spied heading toward Judah. The Ethiopians and Lubims had combined forces, and their huge militia was racing toward Judah bent on its destruction.

Soon Judah was at war, facing one million hostile soldiers. What does a trusting servant of God do when facing such a dilemma? How did Asa react?

"Asa cried unto the Lord his God, and said, Lord, it is nothing with thee to help, whether with many, or with them that have no power: help us, O Lord our God; for we rest on thee, and in thy name we go against this multitude. O Lord, thou art our God; let not man prevail against thee. So the Lord smote the Ethiopians before Asa, and before Judah; and the Ethiopians fled" (14:11-12).

This godly man had been given the most horrible, frightful news. He was facing incomprehensible odds against surviving. I ask you, what does Asa's reaction here say to us, the church, today? The meaning of this passage is clear: *Victory — even impossible victory — is preserved for those who put their trust wholly in the Lord.*

Surely the Lord was pleased with Asa's faith in this crisis. Still, he sent a prophet to warn him: *"Hear ye me, Asa, and all Judah... The Lord is with you, while ye be with him; and if ye seek him, he will be found of you; but if ye forsake him, he will forsake you"* (15:2).

This prophecy to Judah is a warning to the church today: "One glorious victory of faith is not enough."

More great trials will come to pass in the life of every believer. Indeed, the more you seek the Lord, the greater your call, the deeper your walk with him, you're going to encounter further afflictions and sufferings, ever-increasing tests of faith. These will continue until the end, Scripture assures us.

So, what is God's message to us in all of this? Simply the following: *We are not to be shaken in faith when even greater tests come upon us.*

Please know that I do not speak this word to you lightly. What I am preaching in this message has been born from my own personal crucible of great sufferings, hard times and crushing trials of faith.

Don't misunderstand: I am not complaining. I can testify that I have seen the loving hand of God in every trial and tribulation throughout my years. I have watched as my wife, Gwen, and my two daughters have come close to death from cancer. I have endured the death of a granddaughter from cancer. I have seen all my children and grandchildren under attack at various times. And I have gone through personal fiery trials. Through it all, I have experienced eclipses of faith, where the Lord's face seemed completely hidden from me during my ordeal.

Yet, after all these years of afflictions, here I stand, testifying that God has brought me through each trial with peace and his song of victory. Still, this is not the end of the story.

Another terrible crisis arose in Asa's life, and this time the righteous king of Judah lost his faith.

Thirty-six years later, another sudden crisis befell Asa and the nation of Judah. Word came to the king that Jerusalem was being blockaded by an enemy army, cutting off all trade routes and threatening to cripple the economy. Something had to be done quickly or the people would starve. What did King Asa do?

This time he did not go to the Lord. In fact, he didn't even pray or consult his spiritual advisors. Instead, he panicked. He not only put his trust in man but hired his own arch enemy, Benhadad of Syria. Asa stripped the kingdom's treasury of all silver and gold and sent it to Syria with this message: "Here is all of our wealth. It's yours, if you will just deliver me from my attacker."

How utterly tragic when the godly, who have trusted the Lord before the world's eyes, suddenly turn to the flesh in a time of crisis. The world responds with mockery, saying, "Is this what happens after spending years believing in God? Is this how faith ends, in shipwreck? How foolish that you ever believed in God in the first place."

Now the Lord sent another prophet to Asa with this word: *"Because thou hast relied on the king of Syria, and not relied on the Lord thy God, therefore is the host of the king of Syria escaped out of thine hand.... Therefore from henceforth thou shalt have wars"* (2 Chronicles 16:7, 9). Our troubles are always compounded, bringing more chaos and upheaval, when we cast aside our enduring faith.

Here is the key to enduring faith: it is the committing of all things into God's hands.

Enduring faith says to the Lord, "I cast every event, every future success or failure, into your care. And I hold you to your promise to commit all that you are, Lord — all your omniscience and omnipotent strength — to preserve me."

Whenever we face afflictions and persecution, Satan comes whispering fears and lies: "How are you going to make it through this crisis? What will you do now? If God is faithful, how could he allow this to happen to you? How could he put your loved ones at risk this way? What will become of you, your family, your house, your job?"

Enduring faith rises up and answers the enemy's lies: "Devil, you're asking the wrong questions. The question for me right now is not how I'm going to make it. It is not what shall become of me and mine. I have already placed everything — all afflictions, all trials, everything that concerns me — into my loving Father's hands. I have trusted all future events to him. And he has proved himself faithful time after time. He is trustworthy with my future."

With this established in our hearts, the question for us then becomes clear: "How can I love and serve my Lord better? How shall I serve others as myself?" Enduring faith means casting ourselves wholly on the will of God as Jesus describes it in the Sermon on the Mount. Simply put, we are to seek God and his concerns first, and the desires of our heart will then be given to us (see Matthew 6:33).

Enduring faith declares, "I have no will of my own. Rather, *his* will be done. No more personal agenda for me. No more playing God by trying to solve my own problems or those of others. Holy Spirit, keep my mind stayed on my Lord and his promises."

Armed with such faith, we will be ready for whatever the present hour brings. Amen!

Trusting God in the Face of Impossibilities

"Being not weak in faith, (Abraham) considered not his own body now dead, when he was about an hundred years old, neither yet the deadness of Sarah's womb" (Romans 4:19).

The essence of true faith is found in this single verse. God had just promised Abraham he would have a son, one who would become the seed of many nations. Remarkably, Abraham didn't flinch at this promise, even though he was well past the age of siring children. Instead, when Abraham received this word from the Lord, he *"considered not his own body now dead (nor)...the deadness of Sarah's womb."*

To the natural mind, it was impossible for this promise to be fulfilled. But Abraham didn't dwell on any such impossibility. According to Paul, the patriarch gave no thought to how God would keep his promise. He didn't try to reason with God, "But, Lord, I have no seed to plant. And Sarah has no life in her womb to conceive. My wife is past the ability to bear children. So, how will you do it, Lord?" Instead of entertaining such questions, Abraham simply "considered not."

Beloved, when God is at work producing a faith that is tried and better than gold, *he first puts a sentence of death on all human resources*. He closes the door to all human reasoning, bypassing every means of a rational deliverance.

The faith that pleases God is born in a place of deadness.

I'm speaking here of the deadness of all human possibilities. It is a place where man-made plans flourish at first but then die. It is a place where human hopes bring temporary relief but soon crash, adding to a sense of helplessness.

Have you been at this place of deadness? Has it seemed you have no options left? You can't call someone to advise you. The heavens are like brass when you pray, your requests falling to the ground. I declare to you, *this is God at work.* His Spirit is working to get you to stop considering the impossibilities — to stop looking to human ways and means — to stop trying to think your way out of your situation.

Abraham didn't stagger in his faith. Rather, he was *"fully persuaded that, what (God) had promised, he was able also to perform"* (Romans 4:21). He recognized that God is able to *work with nothing*. Indeed, our Lord creates out of a void. Consider the Genesis account: Out of nothing, God created the world. With just a single word, he creates. And he can create miracles for us out of nothing.

When all else fails — when your every plan and scheme have been exhausted — that is the time for you to cast everything on God. It is time for you to give up all confidence in finding deliverance anywhere elsc. Then, once you are ready to believe, you are able to see God not as a potter who needs clay but as a Creator who works from nothing. And, out of nothing that is of this world or its materials, God will work in ways and means you never could have conceived.

Peter writes: *"Let them that suffer according to the will of God commit the keeping of their souls to him in well doing, as unto a* faithful Creator*" (1 Peter 4:19, my emphasis)*.

I am convinced that right now the faith of the body of Christ is under fierce satanic attack.

We know that Satan has always brought intense attacks against God's people, causing awful suffering. For centuries, the blood of martyrs has been spilled. Godly saints like Job have been tried severely. But the onslaught we're seeing today against the faithful is Satan's last stand. All the demonic hordes of hell, Satan's amassed principalities and powers of darkness, are waging an all-out war against the faith of God's saints.

Just as wickedness abounds around the world today, so do the afflictions and trials of God's church. We're seeing an unprecedented barrage of sickness, affliction, trouble after trouble, one problem after another — all of which make an overcoming life seem impossible to any believer. Yet, all we are facing right now is supernatural: *"We wrestle not against flesh and blood, but against principalities, against powers, against the rulers of the darkness of this world, against spiritual wickedness in high places" (Ephesians 6:12)*.

Why is the devil so determined to shake God's righteous ones in our time? It is because he knows his time is short. He failed to bring down Job, he failed to bring down Peter, he failed to bring down generations of martyrs. So now he is determined to bring down the faith of this last generation.

Satan's attacks can become so overwhelming that our faith may experience an eclipse.

Consider what happens during an eclipse: When the earth moves between the sun and moon, it obscures the light. For a time, the sun's rays are interrupted. Something similar can happen with the faith of even the godliest believer. Satan can bring trials that are so intense they seem to block the light that empowers our faith.

Peter suffered a severe eclipse of faith, his belief in Christ seeming to fail. Yet Jesus had clearly warned Peter that an eclipse of his faith was coming. Christ told him, "The rooster will not crow tomorrow until you have denied me three times." Just hours later, Peter's faith was in complete shambles.

I can only imagine what went through the apostle's mind to cause him to curse Christ and lie, saying, "I don't know this Jesus you're talking about." Immediately, Peter's faith went into a total eclipse. It seemed as though the shining sun of faith had been totally extinguished.

Yet Peter's eclipse here is recorded for the comfort and encouragement of all believers who are enduring their own eclipses of faith. Have your trials become so intense you've found yourself in a seemingly impossible situation? Now Satan has planted doubts in your mind: questions about God hearing your cries, doubts about the faithfulness of his promises, questions about the effectiveness of prayer.

I have good news for you: *God is not mad at you.* You may ask: "Doesn't Jesus suffer when we mistrust him? Doesn't the Lord grieve when we waver and question his Word and his faithfulness?" Yes, he does. But those who have failed in faith can still keep their eyes on Jesus.

There is no better example of this than Peter. You see, in spite of his sin, the apostle's faith did *not* ultimately fail. Remember, Jesus had given Peter this word of encouragement at Passover: *"When thou art converted, strengthen thy brethren"* (Luke 22:32). Beloved, this is the Lord's word for you and me as well. He tells us just as he told Peter, "Keep your eyes on me. You are going to come through this. And you're going to help your brothers and sisters in my house."

Later, in the book of Acts, we find Peter locked up in an inner prison. An angel comes to him, shakes off his chains, and tells him to get up and leave. At that point, Peter never looks at the impossibilities around him: the iron gates he had to go through, the many guards and soldiers he had to pass by at his own peril. Instead, Peter rises in faith at the angel's instruction, and when he comes to the iron gates they open of their own accord.

So it will be for you, dear saint, if you are willing to get up and move on in faith. Indeed, I have two special words for all who face impossibilities:

1. A recovery of faith depends on a fuller revelation of the love of our heavenly Father toward us.

"The Lord thy God in the midst of thee is mighty; he will save, he will rejoice over thee with joy; he will rest in his love, he will joy over thee with singing" (Zephaniah 3:17). Here is a glorious revelation of the steadfastness of God's love for his people. Scripture tells us he rests and rejoices in his love for us!

The Hebrew word for "rest" here means God hasn't a single question concerning his love for us. In other words, he has fixed, or settled, his love for us, and he will never take it away. In fact, we're told God is so satisfied in his love for us that he *sings about it.*

In addition, says the apostle Paul, everything that is out of divine order — all that is of unbelief and confusion — is changed by the appearance of God's love. *"After that the kindness and love of God our Savior toward man appeared"* (Titus 3:4). In the preceding verse, Paul says, *"We ourselves also were sometimes foolish, disobedient, deceived"* (3:3). In other words: "Everything was out of order. Our faith was not an overcoming one. But the kindness and love of God appeared, which the Father shed on us abundantly through Christ – and that changed everything."

Beloved, there is no faith that can stand against impossibilities unless everything — every problem, every affliction — is committed into the loving care of our Father. When my situations are at their worst, I must rest in simple faith. I may not see the evidence, but God is at work. Every moment of the day, every hour I sleep, he is making a way for me. And his plan is right on schedule, at all times. What seems to me a delay is his holy work. One day I will look back at these trying times and say, "Lord, now I see. You were there all the time, working my miracle."

2. Never, ever quit praying and crying out to the Lord.

Those who are in despair may be tempted to shut themselves out of communion with God. Yet doing so can be fatal. In Psalm 88, you may find a description of what you are going through. A godly man named Heman tells of his hopeless situation:

"My soul is full of trouble. I have been brought down to the pit, and I am among the dead. God has laid me in the lowest pit in darkness, and his wrath lies hard on me. My friends have forsaken me; I am shut up, closed in. I mourn because of my affliction" (Psalm 88:3-9, my paraphrase). Heman then challenges God: *"Wilt thou shew wonders to the dead? Shall the dead arise and*

praise thee? Shall thy loving kindness be declared in the grave? Or thy faithfulness in destruction? Shall thy wonders be known in the dark? And thy righteousness in the land of forgetfulness?" *(Psalm 88:10-12).*

Heman is saying, in effect, "I need a miracle *now*, Lord, not at the Resurrection. This is my last hope. Soon it will be too late because I'll be dead. You face a deadline here, God. Help me now, or it's too late. Why are you casting me off? Why do you hide your face from me? Why don't you answer my cries?"

This is hopelessness, despair, an apparently impossible crisis. What can a godly soul do? How does a righteous soul react? Like Heman, we are to cry night and day: *"O Lord God of my salvation, I have cried day and night before thee. Let my prayer come before thee: incline thine ear unto my cry. Unto thee have I cried, O Lord; and in the morning shall my prayer prevent thee"* (88:1-2, 13).

Our faith and strength may grow weak. But in our times of weakness, God has given us marvelous promises to renew and strengthen us. Here are some of his promises that sustain me:

◆ *"God is my strength and power: and he maketh my way perfect. He sent from above, he took me; he drew me out of many waters; he delivered me from my strong enemy, and from them that hated me: for they were too strong for me. He is a buckler [protector] to all them that trust in him"* (2 Samuel 22:33, 17, 18, 31).

◆ *"Blessed is the man whose strength is in thee.... They go from strength to strength, every one of them in Zion appeareth before God"* (Psalm 84:5, 7).

Do you believe your God is strong, as the Psalmist declares? If he is, then no power can stand before him. Commit everything into his mighty hand of strength. He will make a way. Most of all, believe his word: *"In the day when I cried thou answeredst me, and strengthenedst me with strength in my soul"* (138:3).

An Eclipse of Faith

Jesus warned Peter: *"Simon, Simon, behold, Satan hath desired to have you, that he may sift you as wheat: but I have prayed for thee, that thy faith fail not: and when thou art converted, strengthen thy brethren. And (Peter) said unto him, Lord, I am ready to go with thee, both into prison, and to death. And he said, I tell thee, Peter, the cock shall not crow this day, before that thou shalt thrice deny that thou knowest me"* (Luke 22:31-34).

Christ's warning here is clear: Satan was about to orchestrate a supernatural attack on Peter's faith. To sift means to "shake violently, up and down, sideways, back and forth, to stir in every way." Simply put, the devil wanted to shake the foundations of this disciples's faith in the severest possible way.

Earlier that day, Peter had boasted of having an unfailing faith. He had said to Jesus in front of the other disciples, "Lord, I will never doubt you. I would die before I ever mistrusted you." Make no mistake: Peter's boast wasn't just froth or mere emotion. Of all the disciples, this man had demonstrated boldness of belief time after time. It was he who stepped out of the boat to take the first few steps on the water toward Jesus. And Peter had declared such faith in Jesus' divinity — saying, "Thou art the Christ, the Son of God" — that Jesus said he would build his church upon this testimony. Peter's belief was real — *and that is the very reason the devil went after him.*

All Christians are tested concerning their faith.

Tests come as the flesh rises up against the spirit to lust after the things of the world. But for some servants, Satan's sifting is much more than a war between flesh and spirit. It is an on-site, face-to-face, supernatural attack by the devil himself to try to destroy their belief. Such servants' faith comes under direct, well-devised attacks by forces of hell, shaking them mentally, physically and spiritually.

Yet few of us could imagine attacks so severe that we would be tempted to deny Jesus. In the previous chapter I referred to Peter's great trial. Now picture Peter standing outside the religious council, warming himself by the fire as Jesus is on trial. I can only imagine the awful things Satan injected into Peter's mind, causing him to wonder: "I can't believe what's happening to Jesus. If he were truly God, how could he allow such humiliation to take place? He's supposed to be the Son of the living God. If he can't deliver himself, how can he deliver me? All the things he told us are going up in smoke. Where is God's power, his presence at this desperate hour?"

I want to show you how God has ordained our faith to come through such severe fires.

A "spiritual eclipse" is that dark hour when God seems to be absent from our lives.

An eclipse of faith happens most often during our times of testing, as Satan moves in to try to obscure our vision of the Lord. Have you ever faced such an eclipse? An hour when your mind was flooded with questions? When your prayers seemed to fall on the ground, and God's Word seemed closed to you? When you felt your life was empty, useless, a total failure?

At such times, you hear whispers of accusation: "After all the praying you've done – all the revelations you've received from God's Word, all your testifying of God's faithfulness — you are still weak. You can't practice what you preach." Suddenly you're tempted to think, "This faith-walk doesn't make sense in my life. None of it adds up for me, and I can't make it work. I don't think I can handle this anymore."

Consider Peter's language in the midst of his eclipse of faith. When someone asked him, "Aren't you a follower of this Jesus?" Peter lied, "I don't know what you're talking about. I don't know who that man is." When pressed about it a second time, he again responded, "I don't know him." Finally, when asked a third time, Peter uttered a curse and screamed, "I've never been with this man!"

Talk about a total eclipse of faith: Peter's thoughts and words made him sound like an enraged atheist.

The disciple's faith was completely shattered. He had crossed a line, actually denying Jesus. This same bold disciple who had cast out demons had now sunk to total unbelief. Some must have thought, "Surely God is finished with Peter, removing his anointing. After all, how could any true servant of God speak this way?"

I'll tell you how it can happen. It occurs when we're under the enemy's heavy barrage and God seems completely absent. That is precisely the time when Satan's voice comes through so loud and clear we lose all sight of the Lord. Suddenly, we feel our life has been spent in vain, that it has counted for nothing. In that dark moment of eclipse, the devil has created such chaos we can't possibly see a way out. We can't imagine God's power being able to deliver us.

Satan had wanted Peter to spin out into total despair. Indeed, the disciple realized to his horror, "I denied Jesus – not just once, but three times. What has happened to me?" Imagine the cloud of condemnation cloaking Peter's mind in that hour.

What about you? Have you lived under condemnation because at one point your faith went into eclipse? Maybe you continually turned to a sinful habit or doubted God's ability to work his promises in your life. Since then you've lived in a spiral of fear, guilt and condemnation.

We all know how God delivered Peter out of this horrible time. He did it the same way he delivered other holy men in Scripture who faced their own eclipse of faith.

Jeremiah also suffered an eclipse of faith.

Here was a powerful preacher of holiness and repentance, a fearless prophet who had the mind of God and walked in the fear of the Lord. Yet as we read Jeremiah 20, we find this man suffering a horrible eclipse of faith.

Jeremiah was preaching at the temple gate when a Satan-possessed priest, Pashur, marched up and slapped his face. Pashur ordered Jeremiah dragged off and locked in a public stock, where he was mocked by the passing crowds. When Jeremiah was finally released, he pronounced God's judgment on Pashur and his followers: *"You, Pashur, and this city are coming down. You're all going into captivity"* (see Jeremiah 20:6).

Immediately, a darkness of soul descended on Jeremiah and he collapsed in discouragement. The once-penetrating holiness preacher now vented dark feelings toward God: *"Lord, you deceived me. The word you gave me has become a reproach. Every day I am ridiculed. You have abandoned me, so I'm quitting you. I'm not going to speak your Word anymore. All your promises are empty. My life and ministry have ended in shame. You should have killed me in the womb"* (see 7:18, 14).

Tell me, did Jeremiah cross a line here? Could such language come out of anyone who claims to serve God? We find our answer in the very next chapter: *"The word of the Lord came to Jeremiah"* (see 21:1). The prophet's eclipse passed and God did not miss a beat. Jeremiah's most effective ministry lay ahead of him.

You see, God is always aware of the devices and attacks Satan uses against his most effective servants. And the Lord knew Jeremiah's faith would endure the eclipse. He knew his servant's cry came out of confusion and pain. And Scripture makes it clear: not for a single moment did God lift his anointing from him.

Most of us can't relate to such severe siftings of faith as Peter and Jeremiah endured.

As we read about Jeremiah here, we may think, "I have never accused God of deceiving me, as Jeremiah did. I have never said to the Lord, 'I quit.' I can't relate to that." Yet this doesn't mean our faith has not experienced an eclipse. Ours may be more hidden. The truth is, we can develop an equally despairing attitude if we feel God has let us down. After a disappointing experience, Satan may implant thoughts like these: "Where is your God now when you need him? Things have gone from bad to worse, but he is nowhere in sight. God promised to make a way of escape for you. So, where is he?"

Though we may not express it outwardly, we entertain thoughts that the Lord is not with us, that he's mad at us, that we aren't measuring up in his eyes. So we give God the silent treatment, backing off from him in prayer and neglecting to trust him in our trials.

I tell you, the devil is absolutely determined to block your vision of God's mercy and grace. Like the moon during an eclipse, he is little by little attempting to cover up your view of Jesus until things become completely dark. You may wonder, "But isn't Jesus right to be offended when we mistrust him? Doesn't it grieve him when we waver and question his faithfulness?" Yes, it does grieve him. And yes, our unbelieving thoughts can lead to confusion and chaos. Bitterness can take root and, if allowed to harden, can lead to a complete falling away.

But the fact remains, God knows the true depths of what is in your heart, and for him nothing has changed about you. He doesn't suddenly see you as his enemy, changing in an instant because of your troubled spirit. He still considers you his friend, a warrior for the kingdom who's on the cusp of moving into new areas of trust. And for that very reason, you have become a target of Satan.

Yet, all along, God has planned for your faith to come through this temporary eclipse.

Many of us can relate to the partial eclipse of faith that David endured.

In Psalm 55, David speaks of a satanic attack that drained all his strength and patience. It caused an eclipse so severe David wanted to run. He moaned, "There is pain in my soul, a pressure that never lets up. It's a battle that never ends. What I am going through terrifies me. There are times I can't stop trembling.

"Lord, don't hide from me anymore. Please, listen to my complaint. You have to make a way of escape for me. If only I had wings like a dove, I would fly out of this place and hide in some wilderness. I just want rest from this battle."

What was the cause of David's awful battle? It was a voice: *"Because of the voice of the enemy"* (Psalm 55:3, my emphasis). In Hebrew, the meaning here is "the voice of a man." It was Satan speaking, along with his demonic oppressors: *"Because of the oppression of the wicked"* (55:3).

David says of these voices, *"They cast iniquity upon me, and in wrath they hate me"* (55:3). In other words: "The tongues of devils are hurling accusations at me. Satan and his henchmen conspire against me, harassing me with lies. They dig up failures from my past and bring them before me, trying to make me fearful."

What did David do about this? He cried out to the Lord for help, asking him to silence the enemy's accusations: *"Destroy, O Lord, and divide their tongues"* (55:9). *"Every day they wrest [twist] my words: all their thoughts are against me for evil.... They mark my steps"* (56:5, 6).

David's testimony makes it clear for all of us: *This is war.* We are facing evil powers in a fight for our faith against the father of lies. And the only way we can do battle is to cry out to the Lord for help.

Like other holy servants of God, David came out of his eclipse and was used mightily as never before.

The same joy that Peter, Jeremiah and David ultimately experienced also awaits us just beyond our eclipse. Indeed, it is when we are at our very lowest — at the deepest point of our unbelief — that God is doing his deepest work in us, preparing us to glorify him.

Like Peter, you may feel utterly defeated. Or, like Jeremiah, you feel God has deceived and abandoned you. Or, like David, you have been drained of all strength and patience. You see no possible way out of your eclipse. I urge you to do three things:

1. Rest in God's love for you. Remember these servants' examples and the plan God had in place for each of them through their trial. They were meant to come out of their eclipse prepared for the ministry God had ready for them.

2. Know that no matter how deep your unbelieving thoughts, the Lord sees what you are going through, and his love for you never wavers. Though we are faithless, he remains faithful: *"We ourselves also were sometimes foolish, disobedient, deceived; after that the kindness and love of God our Savior…appeared"* (Titus 3:3-4).

3. Do as David did and cry to the Lord for help. *"Lord God of my salvation, I have cried day and night before you. In the morning my prayer comes before you. Incline your ear to my cry"* (see Psalm 55).

Dear saint, make this your prayer, as I have made it mine: "Lord, at times I have given you the silent treatment. I have backed away from you because of my disappointments. But I step toward you now in prayer, by faith. Hear my cry, Jesus. I know this is not my battle to fight but yours. I trust you to silence the enemy's tongue. And I know that your love reigns over me, even at my darkest times. I rest in your delight in me."

The High Cost of Mercy

"Love ye your enemies, and do good, and lend, hoping for nothing again; and your reward shall be great, and ye shall be the children of the Highest: for he is kind unto the unthankful and to the evil. Be ye therefore merciful, as your Father also is merciful" (Luke 6:35-36).

Throughout the Bible, a powerful theme rings out: *"The Lord thy God is a merciful God"* (Deuteronomy 4:31). This theme of mercy is at the very core of the Old Testament. We read it again and again in Deuteronomy, Chronicles, Nehemiah and Psalms: "The Lord your God is gracious and merciful." Likewise, we see the same theme of mercy in each of the Gospels and throughout the New Testament.

God paid a high price to show boundless mercy to a sinful world. Think of it: No one can measure Christ's pain at taking upon himself the sins of the world. Yet Scripture does give clear details about the cost Jesus paid for the mercy he ministered here on earth. First, he was rejected by the religious world. The leaders of his day turned on him with outright venom. Moreover, he was mocked and despised by rich and poor, educated and illiterate alike. And his message was refused by all but a few. According to the Psalms, Jesus' name became a song of drunkards. Finally, society spat on him, abused him, nailed him to a cross and killed him.

As the beneficiaries of God's mercy, we know something of the cost to Jesus for extending such mercy to a lost world. After all, his tender mercy found us personally in our sinful bondage. He heard our heart's cry and delivered us. He changed us, opened our eyes, filled us with his Holy Spirit, and made us vessels of honor to proclaim his gospel.

Make no mistake: *It is a costly mercy we have received.* We preach that God's mercy is free, that it is unmerited and therefore of no cost to us. The price for it was paid in full by Christ's shed blood. And, indeed, all of this is true. God is fully satisfied by the price Jesus paid to bring us his mercy. And his mercy provides assurance of eternal life to every true believer.

Yet there is a price on the human side – our side – of God's mercy. What is the cost to us? It is *the high cost of becoming a true witness to the power of the mercy we have received.*

Offering the same mercy shown to us will cost us dearly here on earth.

We can expect to pay this cost in our everyday life. You see, Jesus commands us, *"Be ye therefore merciful, as your Father also is merciful"* (Luke 6:36). And, as Christ showed by example, to be merciful as the Father is merciful is very costly. Jesus paid the price of that mercy in his flesh, and we can expect to pay a great price. Like him, we will face total rejection. As messengers of the gospel, especially, our witness will not be accepted by the world.

In fact, the more Christ is exalted in our lives, the more we can expect to be ridiculed and rejected. He tells us, in essence, "Let my life show you the cost of mercy. It is total rejection by this world." *"Remember the word that I said unto you, The servant is not greater than his lord. If they have persecuted me, they will also persecute you"* (John 15:20).

The apostle Paul testified to this truth: *"(We) labor, working with our own hands: being reviled, we bless; being persecuted, we suffer it: being defamed, we entreat: we are made as the filth of the world, and are the offscouring [scum] of all things unto this day"* (1 Corinthians 4:12-13).

What are we to make of this rejection? Jesus answers us: *"Rejoice ye in that day, and leap for joy: for behold, your reward is great in heaven"* (Luke 6:23). This is a difficult truth to swallow. How can we rejoice and be glad at harsh persecution? It is all part of the high cost of mercy. As it was with Paul, who was seen as scum, so it is for Christ's body, the church. There is a price we all must pay when we preach Jesus and his mercy.

Mercy has broken the chains of all addictions, translating multitudes from the kingdom of Satan into the kingdom of Christ.

When I first came to New York in the 1950s, the drug plague was mostly marijuana and prescription drugs. Heroin didn't have the grip it came to have later. In recent decades, Satan brought in crack and then crystal meth. Now he has introduced new drugs that have greater power to addict: strains of cocaine and heroin from Mexico, Iraq, Colombia and Afghanistan.

Meanwhile, the devil has unleashed an ocean of alcohol upon young people. College and high school campuses have been flooded by a party spirit, with barrels of beer, wine and liquor fueling drunken sprees. Teenagers by the droves are entering secular rehab clinics, while others remain bound by addiction. All of this is the devil's last-ditch effort to enslave masses and "immunize" them to the mercy message of Jesus.

But the mercy of God has amazing power to deliver. There was a time, with millions throughout the world narcotized, that Satan thought he had prevailed. Indeed, word spread throughout the world that once the devil binds you, you are forever hopeless. But in every generation, God sends his Holy Spirit into the highways and byways. And he goes directly to the heart of Satan's territory: into city slums, into crack houses, onto flat rooftops wherever addicts lie in stupors. And mercy has shone upon the weakest, the offscouring, the most drug-crippled, those forgotten and cast aside by society as hopelessly lost.

The first heroin addict to be saved and delivered through the Teen Challenge ministry was Sonny Arguinzoni. Sonny now serves as bishop of more than 600 churches worldwide made up of former addicts. At a conference of these churches, 1,000 former prostitutes formed a choir to sing God's praises for his delivering power. Nicky Cruz, the famous former gangster and graduate of Teen Challenge, has preached the mercy gospel to multiple millions around the world, with multitudes being set free and delivered.

The whole world ought to arise and thank God for his saving deliverance, for restoring those once lost and abandoned by humanity. At the very least, society should thank God for saving drunkard dads and reuniting them with their wives and children. But, I assure you, it will never happen. In every generation, the world has rejected Jesus' power to change lives, even when faced with clear evidence to the contrary.

The fact is *the world will never accept Jesus as the answer*, whether for deliverance or salvation. If Christ is the origin of all liberating mercy – if the mercy of the Cross is the cause of miracles – it will always be cast aside as rubbish. The world is going to call our work a fraud. But we are to remember what Jesus told us: *"When they reproach you, rejoice and leap for joy, because your reward is great in heaven"* (see Luke 6:23).

Living out the Lord's mercy will also cost us a life-changing confrontation concerning the body of Christ.

Before he became the apostle Paul, Saul was the number-one persecutor of Christ's church. Imagine Saul's anguish at Damascus when Jesus confronted him with the reality of his church body. He told Saul, "I am Jesus, your Messiah – and you are persecuting *me*." Saul had thought he was simply dealing with individuals, doing God's work to root out Jewish heretics. He didn't know he was attacking the Lord's own body when he went after the church. Now Saul was jolted with the truth: Everything he had said and done against Christians was felt personally by Jesus himself.

Saul's confrontation with this truth changed his life. As Paul the apostle, he grew to understand how deeply God loved his church. He came to see that, in the Lord's eyes, the church was a costly pearl. It was also a spotless bride for his Son – one corporate, invisible body made up of blood-purchased children from every tribe and nation on earth.

I am convinced we today do not take this truth as seriously as we should. If we fully understood it, it would mean the end of all grudges in the church, the end of all bitterness, the end of all prejudice, fleshly competition, pride, gossip and division. Right now, the world needs a living example of the costly mercy of Christ. Tensions have never been greater. For decades in many nations, tribe has warred against tribe. These tribal wars have brought about poverty, disease and broken families, and have bred raging hatred in new generations. Meanwhile, in Europe and the United States, racial tension is sweeping through society, even creeping into churches.

The costly mercy that's needed throughout the world can only come from those who have tasted and received such mercy for themselves. And that is the costly calling of the church of Jesus Christ. It is to offer a mercy that lays down self for the sake of a brother or sister – and, as Jesus demonstrated, even for an enemy.

I exhort you to stop here and confront this truth in your own life.

Go no further in your life or ministry – stop all your plans and good works – until you confront the implications of being a member of Christ's body. The Lord declares of his church, "This is my pearl of great price, the bride for my Son." Think of what a miracle it is to be a part of such a body. Think too of the great calling of this body to show mercy to an unmerciful world.

When Paul famously wrote to the Corinthians, it was to a church that had turned against him. Yet, as Paul thought of this church as Christ's body, he wrote, "You have become very dear to me. You all have my heart. I love you and appreciate each of you."

Simply put, *mercy looks beyond faults and failures, beyond self-justification.* If we truly believe that we wound Christ personally whenever we wound a brother or sister – that what we say and do against a single member of his body is, as Jesus said, "against me" – we would not rest until we were clear of it all.

Yet, the truth is, we can mistreat others. We can separate ourselves from a brother or sister. We can say and think racial words and thoughts. We can easily misrepresent others. And we think it is "just between God and me." So we confess it to the Lord and repent, then go our way thinking all is well. Yet we never give thought to how we have wounded Jesus – or our brother – in the process. We've not only wounded a brother, we have wounded *the Lord*. Indeed, we did it to the whole body, because if one hurts, all hurt.

Here is the revelation we are given: "I belong to the body of Christ! And so does my brother, my sister. We are all one. That solves all gossip, all tension, all grudges, because we are connected to the head."

I leave you with the same message Paul delivered to his fellow workers.

Paul wrote to the church:

◆ *"Let nothing be done through strife or vainglory; but in lowliness of mind let each esteem other better than themselves. Look not every man on his own things, but every man also on the things of others"* (Philippians 2:3-4).

◆ *"I beseech (you)…be of the same mind in the Lord"* (4:2).

◆ *"Put on therefore, as the elect of God, holy and beloved, bowels of mercies, kindness, humbleness of mind, meekness, longsuffering; forbearing one another, and forgiving one another, if any man have a quarrel against any: even as Christ forgave you, so also do ye. And above all these things put on charity, which is the bond of perfectness"* (Colossians 3:12-14).

Here is how Paul sums it all up – indeed, here is mercy lived out in full: *"Because ye (are) dear unto us"* (1 Thessalonians 2:8). I ask you: are all your brothers and sisters in Christ dear to you? As the life of our Lord flows to us, the members of his body, we begin to love not only each other but even our enemies.

Lord, let us be merciful as you have been merciful to us!

A Time to Weep and a Time to Fight

We All Need a Word from God to See Us Through Perilous Times.

As I read through the Old Testament, I find my faith greatly encouraged by the example David set. An awful calamity struck this man, causing his very life to be threatened by those closest to him. I am awed by David's determination to get a word from God in the midst of his perilous time.

Here is the scene: David and his band of 600 loyal men were on the run from King Saul, who had been trying to kill him. At one point the small army encamped in a town called Ziklag, where they settled their families. From there they went out to do battle, leaving their wives and children safely behind.

After one battle, David and his army were making a three-day trip back home when their village was suddenly raided by the Amalekites. This fierce enemy kidnapped the families of David and his men and burned down the whole town. Imagine the scene as David's army returned: *"So (they) came to the city, and behold, it was burnt with fire, and their wives, and sons, and their daughters were taken captive"* (1 Samuel 30:3).

These mighty men must have been struck mute as they discovered what had happened. It was so sudden and catastrophic they couldn't take it all in. I picture them walking about stunned and bewildered, crying out in agony, "How could this happen? Why would God allow it?" *"Then David and the people that were with him lifted up their voice and wept, until they had no more power to weep"* (30:4).

This scene from David's life shows us there is most certainly a time to weep when calamity strikes. Scripture describes David's soldiers as "mighty men," implying battle-hardened men who didn't cry. But this calamitous event had brought the strong men to great weeping.

After all, it was no small disaster. It wasn't just the loss of homes, cattle or crops that caused David's mighty men to weep; they would soon get over that. Rather, it was the threat to their beloved wives and children that pierced their very souls. And what followed this scene could have been even more disastrous for David: *"David was greatly distressed; for the people spake of stoning him, because the soul of all the people was grieved"* (30:6).

What we are witnessing in the world today is described in Scripture as "the day of the Lord's vengeance, and the year of recompences for the controversy of Zion" (Isaiah 34:8).

I believe that through all the churning and chaotic events going on in the world today, God is bringing down greed, covetousness and pride. I'm convinced he could no longer permit sexual perversions to destroy the soul of an entire generation.

And I believe same-sex marriages have become a flash point of God's vengeance.

The period of history that Isaiah describes is one full of weeping, fear and trembling. Yet the Lord gave Isaiah a word of assurance for his people: *"Strengthen ye the weak hands, and confirm the feeble knees. Say to them that are of a fearful heart, Be strong, fear not: behold, your God will come with vengeance, even God with a recompence; he will come and save you"* (Isaiah 35:3-4).

The Lord was saying, in essence: "Strengthen the exhausted. Build up those who are weak among you. Encourage all who are afraid and full of anxiety. Tell them, 'There is no need to be fearful. This is all the Lord's doing. And through it, he is going to preserve his people. *He is doing this to save you.*'"

Beloved, even the most godly among us experience a trembling of heart, a sudden rush of fear, when a terrible crisis comes. At such a time, it isn't a sin to have a sudden moment of deep anxiety. Indeed, when the Lord gave this word to Isaiah, he was making sure that all who felt overwhelmed by the terrifying situation would not be crushed by it. He wanted every weary, troubled heart to hear: "Fear not! Take courage, for the Lord is a Savior to his people."

After enduring a period of weeping, there comes a time to fight.

A time comes when all weeping must end. It is then God's people are to rise above their grieving, above every dire foreboding, and *get back their fight*. In the New Testament, Hebrews echoes Isaiah's words: *"Strengthen the hands that are weak and the knees that are feeble, and make straight paths for your feet,* so that the limb which is lame may not be put out of joint, but rather be healed" (Hebrews 12:12-13, NAS).

The meaning here is, in effect: "Don't stay down. Get up and fight for your faith. Exercise your trust in the Lord. Don't give in to sore, trembling knees. Instead, keep running. If you succumb to fear and worry, your faith may end up crippled."

Consider the crippling response of David's army to their calamity. After these mighty men had finished weeping, they grew outraged. They blamed David for having allowed the disaster. They were so out of joint, so embittered by their horrible misfortune, they began picking up stones to kill him.

In my opinion, this is exactly what the majority of people are doing right now over the current economic calamity. Many are blinded by their outrage. They're turning left and right asking, "Who is to blame for the calamity? Throw them all in jail!"

I urge every follower of Jesus: Forget about how we got here. Forget about who is responsible. Most of all, forget about your own personal what-ifs: "If only I had done this or that, my finances would be okay." If you hang onto such thoughts, your fear will turn into rage or some other crippling, destructive spirit. The Lord intends a different direction for all your energies. His Word tells us, "Now is the time to fight for your faith."

Consider David's response to his calamity: He encouraged himself. "David encouraged himself in the Lord" (1 Samuel 30:6). Instead of giving in to fear, David decided to fight his fears. I believe he did this by remembering all of God's past deliverances in his life. In his young life, David had killed a bear, slain a lion and brought down the giant Goliath. Now he recounted those battles and the many others he had won. Every victory had been brought about because of his unwavering faith.

David was saying, "I need a word from the Lord." He knew no one could encourage him – not his priest, Abiathar, not the very wise captains under his charge, indeed no counselor at all. David had to have a word himself directly from the One who had delivered him from every calamity he had faced.

Beloved, the same is true for you and me today. There simply is nobody on earth who can lift your soul out of despair. No one can keep your spirit encouraged through the duration of your crisis. *We all have to get our own word from the Lord.* Like David, we are called to strengthen ourselves by recalling God's deliverances in our lives. And we must also remember those times when God has proven fruitful in past generations.

Our encouragement to each other can only go so far.

If the sermons you hear by your pastor are anointed, they will produce life in you. The preaching of God's Word will always encourage his saints. Likewise, corporate worship will lift you for a season. But how quickly we forget that uplift after a Sunday service is over. As Monday and Tuesday pass and the news begins to turn bad, we often fall back into fits of anxiety and fear.

In normal times, I am able to draw advice from my godly wife, Gwen. She is always there to give me a good word, just what I need. I feel toward her the way David did when he said to Abigail, *"See, I have hearkened to thy voice"* (1 Samuel 25:35). But things can be different in calamitous times. When our faith is being threatened – indeed, when our very lives are being threatened – the counsel of spouses, pastors and wise friends can only take us so far.

Today we are living in fearful times such as few of us have ever known. The truth is, only a personal word from the Lord can lead us through such times with the enduring hope we need. And God has always been faithful to provide a word to his people throughout history.

In the Old Testament we read this phrase over and again: *"The word of the Lord came..."* Scripture says of Abraham: *"After these things the word of the Lord came unto Abram"* (Genesis 15:1). We read of Joshua: *"According unto the word of the Lord which he (gave) Joshua"* (Joshua 8:27). And so it was with David and the prophets also. We read of them, *"The word of the Lord came unto..."*

As for God's people today, we have the abiding Holy Spirit to speak a word from heaven to us. Through him, the comforting, healing, guiding word of the Lord is available to all who trust in him.

Consider the 600 soldiers who followed David. They heard the word that God gave their leader. But that word had to be made real to each of those soldiers individually. It had to be something spoken by God to their own spirits so they also could begin to fight back.

Likewise today, I believe the challenge for all believers is to stay in the Scriptures until the Holy Spirit makes God's promises seem to jump off the pages *to them personally*. We can know when that happens because we will hear the still, small voice of the Spirit whispering: "This promise is yours. It is God's Word given just to you, to see you through these hard times."

I am convinced you can't fight the battle of faith without hearing the assuring voice of the Lord *to you*.

David encouraged himself, got back his fight and immediately acted in faith.

When David got back his fighting spirit, he sent for something known as the ephod. This was a kind of garment that included two stones kept in the priest's breastplate. On occasion God spoke through the ephod. And David was determined to get a word of direction from the Lord.

"David said to Abiathar the priest...I pray thee, bring me hither the ephod. And Abiathar brought thither the ephod to David. And David inquired at the Lord, saying, Shall I pursue after this troop? Shall I overtake them?" (1 Samuel 30:7-8).

Consider what David did here. After he had wept, and after he had regained his fight, this man went directly to his knees. The Lord gave him the word of direction he needed: *"He answered him, Pursue: for thou shalt surely overtake them, and without fail recover all"* (30:8). God's direction to David was, "Go forth. You will be victorious." In other words: "Fight on!"

In the very next verse we read, *"So David went, he and the six hundred men that were with him"* (30:9). David quickly acted on the word God had given him. Yet, I wonder, how did David know where to go? What direction did he know to take so he could recover all?

I believe there was a voice behind David whispering, "This is the way, walk in it." And, beloved, the same is true for us today. Many churches sing the uplifting gospel song, "He Will Make a Way," and our Lord does just that. You see, he had a plan in place for each of us before our present calamity fell. And his plan is still at work even now through all the turmoil we face.

I'm convinced the word that David played over and over in his mind was, *"You will recover all."* David knew full well he wouldn't recover his house in Ziklag. None of his soldiers would recover their homes, their gardens, their possessions. Those things were all gone. No, the "all" they were going to recover was *the safety and security of their families.*

Do you see the parallels to our own time? These men weren't about to recover a past lifestyle. They weren't about to return to the same quiet, placid days that had been so peaceful before. Those "good old days" were now history.

But that wasn't what mattered to David and his 600 mighty men. All they cared about was that their families – the only things that truly mattered – were going to be safe. They may have had to live in tents with their wives and children after that. But God had assured them they were going to be secure.

God didn't tell David how he was going to deliver him and his family.

Beloved, the Lord isn't going to explain to us how he will provide for our loved ones. He won't show us how he's going to keep us safe in the worst of times. His ways are so unusual, so unimaginable, we would never be able to figure them out in a lifetime.

As for David, his deliverance came through an unlikely source: a dying young Egyptian. This servant boy was half-dead when David found him in a wilderness and fed him and gave him water. As David asked the young man, "Who are you?" I think God whispered, "David, he is your deliverance." How unlikely, how miraculous are his ways! It was this nearly dead Egyptian boy who would point the way for David's army to the enemy encampment. In short, God used a nameless boy to lead his people to recover all.

In closing, let me take you again to Isaiah 35:4, *"Say to them that are of a fearful heart, Be strong, fear not: behold, your*

God will come with vengeance, even God with a recompence; he will come and save you."

While the world is under vengeance – when all things seem to be spinning completely out of control – God is in the process of saving us. He is using even the chaos of world events to bring about his salvation. He is faithful to save and to keep his people, through every calamity.

"Trust in the Lord, and do good; so shalt thou dwell in the land, and verily thou shalt be fed" (Psalm 37:3).

God's People Will Not Be Ashamed in the Time of Calamity

When I began working on this message, the *Wall Street Journal* reported that the entire world had come under a great cloud of fear. People in all nations are now paralyzed by world events. Immediately, my thoughts turned to our parishioners at Times Square Church. They show no such fear. Instead, while we all have a great soberness about these times, we also have a deep, abiding joy.

I was led to Psalm 37, written by David: *"The Lord knoweth the days of the upright: and their inheritance shall be for ever. They shall not be ashamed in the evil [calamitous] time: and in the days of famine they shall be satisfied"* (Psalm 37:18-19). Here is an amazing prophecy for God's people, and it is being fulfilled before our eyes.

In short, Psalm 37 tells us the Lord rises up to action against societies whose sins have outraged heaven. David prophesies, *"The arms [power] of the wicked shall be broken"* (37:17). Yet this same Psalm is also one of great hope. It contains an incredible promise to those who put their trust fully in the Lord.

First, there comes a time when God can no longer endure the greed, covetousness and wicked fraud that evil men perpetrate on the poor and needy. David's prophecy speaks of a sudden loss of financial power: *"The wicked shall perish and the enemies of the Lord shall be as the fat of lambs: they shall consume; into smoke shall they consume away"* (37:20). The implication here is that fire will suddenly consume the wealth of the powerful. Riches will quickly spatter into smoke like fat in flames.

Talk about a picture of what has happened to America's economy. In two weeks' time, more than $4 trillion of American wealth vanished. Now we are being told trillions more will go up in smoke. Stock markets all over the world have gone into shock over the news, with brokers weeping and wailing.

I won't go into the reasons why I believe God had to act. But I can say this: We know our God is not asleep. There comes a time Isaiah describes as *"the day of the Lord's vengeance, and the year of recompences for the controversy of Zion"* (Isaiah 34:8). *"I have spread out my hands all the day unto a rebellious people, which walketh in a way that was not good, after their own thoughts; a people that provoketh me to anger continually to my face... I will not keep silence, but will recompence"* (65:2-3, 6).

What we see happening to our economy is not only God's vengeance. It has to do with the very honor and glory of Almighty God. He will not stand by as his ways are maligned by the wicked. Ezekiel writes, *"The time has come, the day has arrived. Let not the buyer rejoice nor the seller mourn; for wrath is against all their multitude.... They have blown the trumpet and made everything ready, but no one is going to the battle; for my wrath is against all their multitude"* (Ezekiel 7:12, 14, NAS). In the midst of wickedness, God has sounded the trumpet of alarm, but the warning has been ignored.

Paul also describes our time when he writes, *"In the last days perilous times shall come.... Evil men and seducers shall wax worse and worse, deceiving, and being deceived"* (2 Timothy 3:1, 13). Think of the huge mortgage companies that seduced and deceived the poor, the unlearned and the unemployed. These unwitting people were lured to sign up for mortgages they could never pay, and when payday came they were left without homes. Reputable banks failed because of the deception, but their executives bailed out with "golden parachutes" of multiple millions.

I read about one such executive throwing an expensive party, dancing the night away with liquor flowing, knowing full well his company was going down. He and others partied wildly despite knowing that hundreds of thousands of people would lose their homes. It is a clear fulfillment of the prophecy in Zephaniah 1:9, *"(They) leap on the threshold [of the poor], which fill their masters' houses."*

How long did we think God would put up with such madness, such mockery of his name? The Lord has the final word on the matter, and he says, *"In the same day also will I punish (them)"* (1:9). In short: "I will put them to shame." *"Their sword shall enter their own heart, and their bows [wealth] shall be broken"* (Psalm 37:15). Even now, as I write this, two billionaires are being bailed out because their wealth vanished overnight.

At the same time the Lord is recompencing the ungodly, he will reward those who trust him.

Here is the theme of my message: *"The Lord upholdeth the righteous.... They shall not be ashamed in the evil time [of calamity]" (Psalm 37:17, 19)*. You may ask, "What does this mean exactly?" It means simply this: God is faithful not just in his recompence of woes, but also in his promises. David is saying, in effect, "Look around you and see how God keeps his Word. His warnings are now being manifested in your headlines, his actions all over your media. I ask you, will not God also keep his Word to preserve his chosen ones?"

Think of it: No matter what happens in the world – no matter how fearful the news becomes, how severely the world shakes, how economies may teeter toward collapse – God's people will not be left ashamed. Indeed, the Lord will act on our faith to fulfill his Word to us. We may suffer, but he will come through for all who fully trust in him. The world will never be able to say, "Your God didn't keep his Word."

Make no mistake, we are going to face impossibilities in the days ahead. But our Lord says he is God of the impossible, providing miracles when there is no human answer. In fact, he willingly puts his reputation in the hands of his people, calling us to commit him to his Word. You may think, "But God can defend his own name. He doesn't need me." Not so! God has chosen his people to be his testimony to a numb, unmoved world. And he is calling us to openly commit him to do what he promises.

You see, in the world's eyes God is always on trial. Unbelievers are watching every time we face impossible situations. They say, "This person sings about God making a way to deliver him. Now we'll see if his God answers him. Will he make it through, or will he end up in shame?"

Skeptics in Jesus' day said similar things at the Crucifixion: "This man boasted his Father would raise him from the dead. Now we'll see. Will it be resurrection or shame?" Jesus wasn't deaf to those taunts. But he knew something they didn't: His Father would never allow him to be put to shame. God would not fail to deliver him *for his own name's sake.*

There are times when it looks as if God hasn't shown up, when his people will be left in shame and despair, but the full story hasn't been told. (The Cross was one of those times.) What we don't realize in the midst of the crisis is that God's own honor is at stake. And throughout the Bible he had a people whose flint-like faith proved his faithfulness in the most difficult times. These servants unashamedly committed the Lord to act, putting his honor at stake while trusting him to deliver.

1. Consider Moses' example at the Red Sea.

Here was a humanly impossible situation. Israel was on the run from the Egyptian army, hemmed in on one side by the sea and by mountains on the other. It was here Moses committed God to his promises. He had already prophesied God would lead Israel into the Promised Land. Now the Lord's reputation was at stake for all to see.

I can hear the reports getting back that Pharaoh had Israel trapped. All of Egypt expected to see the Israelites brought back in chains. Parades would be planned to celebrate Pharaoh's victory, with golden idols exalted over the God of Israel. What was Moses' reaction to this crisis? Facing the vast sea before him, he cried, "Move forward!" Moses so believed in God's care, trusting his word to lead Israel into his promise, he declared, "I know the Lord is faithful. And I'm going to act on his word."

Think about the consequences of such faith. If the Red Sea didn't open up miraculously, Moses would be thought a fool. The Israelites would go back into bondage, and God would never again be trusted. Yet we all know what happened: As Moses stretched out his hand, the waters divided, and the people walked across on dry ground. I tell you, no one who fully trusts in God will ever be put to shame. He will deliver on his promise "for his own name's sake."

2. Consider Joshua.

For six days Israel had marched around the impenetrable city of Jericho, saying, "These walls are coming down." To the people inside Jericho, this sounded absolutely foolish. They must have laughed in derision. Then finally, on the seventh day, God's people were commanded to march not just once but seven times. At this point, even the Israelites must have felt foolish. They might have thought, "Nothing happened the first six days. Now this seems desperate. We'll be shamed if those walls don't fall."

But such thoughts never entered Joshua's mind. He said, "I know what I heard from the Lord, and I know he is able." He committed God to his promise, putting his glory on the line. We know what happened: *"The people shouted when the priests blew with the trumpets: and it came to pass...that the wall fell down flat, so that the people went up into the city, every man straight before him, and they took the city"* (Joshua 6:20). When God's children commit him to his word, he will never let them be shamed.

3. Consider the Hebrew children.

Daniel said the three Hebrew children refused to bow in worship before Nebuchadnezzar's 90-foot gold idol. They stood resolute even when condemned to die in a fiery furnace. As the wicked king taunted, *"Who is that God that shall deliver you out of my hands?" (Daniel 3:15),* the young men committed the Lord to his promises:

"O Nebuchadnezzar, we are not careful to answer thee in this matter. [We don't hesitate in our response.] If it be so, our God whom we serve is able to deliver us from the burning fiery furnace... But if not, be it known unto thee, O king, that we will not serve thy gods, nor worship the golden image which thou hast set up" (3:16-18). They were so confident God would honor his name, they willingly faced certain death.

Prominent leaders from throughout the land gathered for the execution: princes, governors, judges, rulers from surrounding provinces. And Nebuchadnezzar ordered the fire stoked seven times hotter than usual, a heat so fierce it killed the servants tending the furnace. The crowds were aghast, exclaiming, "These men can't survive. They'll drop dead before they get near that furnace. No God can deliver from this kind of fate." Again, the Lord's name was on the line. If he didn't intervene, his name would be defamed throughout the nations.

But the Lord never puts to shame those who fully trust him. Scripture says Jesus himself showed up in that furnace to protect and comfort his servants. And out of the fire walked the three Hebrew children, without even a whiff of smoke on them.

4. Consider King Hezekiah.

Scripture says Hezekiah was God-fearing: *"He clave to the Lord" (2 Kings 18:6).* During Hezekiah's reign, Jerusalem was besieged by the Assyrians, the great world power of the day. This vast army had already captured Samaria and the cities of Judah, and now they surrounded Jerusalem. Their captain stood taunting, "We have overpowered the gods of all nations. How do you expect your God to deliver you?"

Once again, the Lord himself was on trial. His faithfulness was being questioned before the whole empire, before Israel's enemies, even before God's people. What if he didn't act? What if, in the morning, a barrage of arrows came cascading over the city walls? The heathen would gloat, and God's Word would be meaningless.

As the crisis mounted, Isaiah stood by watching it all. He had received a word from the Lord, and he trusted in it fully. Now he committed God to that word, putting the Lord's reputation on the line. He prayed, in essence, "God, my honor doesn't matter. If you don't deliver, I can always hide in the wilderness. It's *your* honor that is at stake."

With that, Isaiah calmly told Hezekiah to tell the Assyrian captain: *"He shall not come into this city, nor shoot an arrow there, nor come before it with shield, nor cast a bank against it. By the way that he came, by the same shall he return, and shall not come into this city, saith the Lord. For I will defend this city, to save it,* for mine own sake"* (19:32-34, my emphasis)*.

God will never let his trusting people be put to shame, and that night he delivered a powerful miracle. Scripture says 185,000 Assyrian soldiers died mysteriously, causing a huge panic, and the mighty army fled. Once again, God defended his people *for his own sake.*

5. Consider Peter and John in the New Testament.

As the two disciples walked toward the temple, they came upon a beggar who had been lame from birth. Peter and John had probably passed this man many times before, but this time they stopped. The throngs in the marketplace heard Peter tell the beggar, *"Look on us.... In the name of Jesus Christ of Nazareth rise up and walk"* (Acts 3:4, 6).

Peter was calling on the Lord to act, with God's own glory at stake. The crowds must have said to each other, "What a foolish preacher. He's asking a man who's been crippled all his life to stand up and walk." I believe those people were ready to laugh Peter and John to scorn.

Then a strange feeling started in the lame man's feet. First he wiggled his ankle. Then the feeling moved upward into his calves and his thighs. He began to crouch, then slowly he pushed himself upright and stood. To the crowd's amazement, the man began to leap and dance.

I ask you: what if God hadn't acted? That was never a concern to Peter, who gladly committed his God to deliver. The Lord will never put those who trust him to shame!

We today are also called to place God's honor, glory and reputation on the line.

Think about these biblical episodes. In each one, everything that Christ came to earth and died for was at stake. Yet all through the Old and New Testaments, God's plan, purpose and people survived. And in every case, God called his children not only to trust him but to believe him to work miracles. Tell me, would the Lord ask any less of our generation?

Consider the testimony we have put forth about our glorious Lord. We have said he will provide, calling him Jehovah Jireh. We have declared his promises to supply for his children. Now, once more, his name and honor are at stake. If we will commit him to act, he promises: *"I wrought for my name's sake, that it should not be polluted before the heathen, in whose sight I brought (Israel) out"* (Ezekiel 20:14). He's saying, in essence, "When I delivered Israel, it wasn't in some hidden corner. I worked miracles for them before the whole world. Now I want to do the same in your generation."

Dear saint, are you facing a situation you have not yet committed to God? Are you being called to put your faith out on a limb in the distant unknown? Have you resolved, "Only a miracle from the Lord can deliver me"? We may not figure out how God will work his deliverance; no one in the Bible did. But we do know this: Just one of his angels can put 185,000 men to flight. The Lord will never let his people be ashamed!

Right now, he is telling us just as he told Israel, "I called you out of your sins. And I have set you within sight of everyone around you, that I may glorify my name. It was I who called you out. And I will deliver you in the sight of the ungodly, for my name's sake." So, will you now walk in what you preach and claim to believe? Will you commit God to his Word for his name to be glorified before multitudes?

May we all adopt the prayer of David for these times: *"Do thou for me, O God the Lord,* for thy name's sake: *because thy mercy is good, deliver thou me"* (Psalm 109:21, my emphasis). God will never put his trusting people to shame. He will keep his Word to you because his own honor is at stake.

The Ever-Increasing Demands of Faith

What is it about faith that keeps demanding of us greater testings? Why do our afflictions grow more intense, more severe, the closer we get to Christ? Just when we come through one trial that proves us faithful, our heart declaring, "Lord, I'll trust you for everything," here comes another test, increased in its intensity.

This experience is shared by Christians all over the world. I see it in all my travels, from continent to continent, and our ministry regularly receives letters from readers who testify of a growing intensity in their trials. A godly pastor friend told me recently, "I have never loved Jesus more than I do today. And yet I have never been so severely tested. My present trial has left me stunned, speechless. I've never felt so helpless, so lacking in wisdom, and I see no human way out of my difficulties. I find myself longing for heaven, for rest from all of this conflict."

The fact is, every saint who grows ever closer to God's heart will find his burdens and trials becoming ever more intense. I call this experience *the ever-increasing demands of faith.* It is a pattern we see throughout Scripture.

Consider the ever-increasing demands on Abraham's faith.

By the time Abraham turned 100 years old, he had endured a lifetime of incredible tests of faith. And through it all he had trusted the Lord. God said of this faithful man, *"I know him, that he will command his children and his household after him, and they shall keep the way of the Lord, to do justice and judgment"* (Genesis 18:19).

In his old age, Abraham was finally given the son promised to him by God. Isaac's name means "laughter," and for a season this boy's name seemed to describe Abraham's life. Every indication is that Abraham enjoyed his later years free from trials. Indeed, God seemed to have given this very old man a furlough from testing.

Yet once again we read, *"It came to pass after these things, God did tempt [test] Abraham"* (22:1). After all the many years of struggles – all the afflictions, the testings, the ever-increasing demands on his faith – godly Abraham faced the most incredible demand yet on his faith. God told the patriarch, *"Take now thy son, thine only son, Isaac, whom thou lovest, and get thee into the land of Moriah; and offer him there for a burnt offering"* (22:2).

As I read this, my human reasoning cries out: "Lord, this man has already been tested to the limit. He doesn't have to prove his faith. You already know his heart! He's at such a wonderful place in life right now. Why does he have to endure another test? Besides, who is going to benefit from his trial? Who among

Abraham's generation will even hear of this test, taking place on an isolated mountain? You know Abraham is going to trust you through it. He has a record of prayer and trust with you in all things. So, what is this trial about?"

You know the story: God spared Isaac, substituting a ram for the sacrifice. And the Lord told Abraham: *"Now I know that thou fearest God, seeing that thou hast not withheld thy son, thine only son from me.... Because thou hast done this thing...I will bless thee... In thy seed shall all the nations of the earth be blessed; because thou hast obeyed my voice"* (Genesis 22:12, 16-18). God told him, in effect, "I know now that you will never hold anything back from me, even your precious son. I know I am everything to you, Abraham. And because you have proven this, I am going to bless you."

Hear what the Spirit is saying to his people in this passage: "Others may never learn about your ever-increasing tests of faith. You may suffer in isolation, alone, with no one to benefit from your testimony of faith and endurance. In fact, you may be judged for your suffering, as others think, 'Why is he going through all this? What sin has he committed to bring this suffering on himself?' Yet you can know the God who led you into your trial of faith knows what your trial means. Your tears have all been bottled by him, every pain felt in his heart. And he assures you: 'This will end in blessing. It will impact those in your family.'"

Abraham was already in glory when these promises were fulfilled by the Lord. But his family, the nation of Israel, and eventually the entire church of Jesus Christ would benefit from his proven faith. Likewise, you may not be there to witness it when God blesses your children and spiritual children. But the Lord makes clear to every servant who endures with faith in him: "This will all end in blessing."

Is there a point in our walk with God when we become so proven faithful through years of testing that we can expect a respite from spiritual warfare?

Is there ever a vacation from troubles, a time when we can relax free of trials? Does a lifetime of meeting faith's demands earn us a furlough from the battle? Is it possible to have nothing left to prove, to reach a point in faith where a test is no longer necessary? The answer, according to Scripture, is a simple, "No." In fact, the opposite is true: the trials of the faithful increasingly become more severe and troublesome. The Bible bears this out again and again from the Old Testament to the New.

Consider David's example. In 1 Chronicles 21, we find David as an elderly saint. At this point Scripture says he is utterly loved by God, admired by angels, a proven man of great faith. As I consider this picture, my human reasoning speaks to me: "David has been in the fires of affliction long enough. Time after time, he has fought till he dropped. His life is an established testimony to your faithfulness. Please, God, give this man a furlough. Let him enjoy time with his grandchildren. You already know his heart. Why can't you let him retire in peace? Let there be no more warfare for such a faithful man."

Was this God's plan for his beloved servant? Not at all. Instead, we read, *"Satan stood up against Israel, and provoked David to number Israel"* (1 Chronicles 21:1). David, in an act of pride, conducted a census to learn how populous Israel had become. For a man who had lived his entire life by faith in the Lord, this was purely an act of flesh – and God was displeased over it. David now faced the worst affliction of his life. A plague swept through Israel, causing the deaths of 70,000 men. When David realized this was happening because of his sin, he fell on his face in anguished repentance. He prayed without ceasing, casting himself solely on God's mercy, and the Lord stopped the plague.

Again, I have to wonder: Why did God allow Satan to have such access to a proven, praying man? Why test the faith of an elderly saint who was already close to death? What could God possibly have been after in David? I'm convinced this same question enters the minds of many godly saints about their own faithful lives: "Lord, you know my heart. I have trusted you through years of excruciating trials. You and I both know I'll trust you no matter what. So, what are you after? Why this awful trial?"

I have two responses to this question, both drawn from what I see in Scripture.

1. *The life of faith continually demonstrates humankind's need for the Lord in all things.* Simply put, we never reach a point of *not needing God.* The idea of a "furlough from trials" presumes a "furlough from *need.*" And there will never be a time when our needs are met by our circumstances. The Lord is our source, our all in all.

The Bible shows us instance after instance when Israel's needs were met and the people stopped relying on God. They became preoccupied with being provided for, when God had already promised to supply all their needs. As Jesus tells us, our purpose is not to seek having our needs met, but to feed on every word that proceeds from the mouth of God (see Matthew 4:4).

2. *I am convinced an additional reason behind our ever-increasing afflictions goes far beyond anything having to do with this world.* From what I read in Scripture, God's elect are being prepared for ministries in glory. And our trials today are meant to bring victories having to do with the Lord's purposes in eternity. This is most clearly demonstrated in the life of the apostle Paul. In him we find our New Testament example of the ever-increasing demands of faith.

We all have read about the perils Paul faced.

In 2 Corinthians 11:24-28 Paul lists all the afflictions he endured, both "without" and "within": *"Five times I received from the Jews the forty lashes minus one. Three times I was beaten with rods, once I was stoned, three times I was shipwrecked. I spent a night and a day in the open sea, and I have been constantly on the move. I have been in danger from rivers, from bandits, from my own countrymen, from Gentiles, from false brothers; in danger in the city, in the country, at sea. I have labored and toiled and often gone without sleep. I have known hunger and thirst and gone without food. I have been cold and naked. Besides everything else, I face daily the pressure of my concern for all the churches"* (my paraphrase).

Paul stated that none of these outward afflictions moved him, and his life proved it. Every time he was about to enter another city, the Holy Spirit reminded him about the chains and afflictions awaiting him. Paul says, in short, "My mere presence stirs things up wherever I go. I face intense physical suffering in every city. A messenger of Satan has been appointed to harass me." Yet he could endure it all, he said, because *"neither count I my life dear unto myself"* (Acts 20:24).

Here in Acts 20, Paul was nearing the last few laps of his race. He had fought a good fight and kept the faith, and now he was leaving Ephesus to go to Jerusalem. As he said goodbye to the Ephesian believers, he told them, "You shall see my face no more." Paul then prophesied over these Christians a deeply painful message, through tears of anguish: *"I know this, that after my departing shall grievous wolves enter in among you, not sparing the flock. Also of your own selves shall men arise, speaking perverse things, to draw away disciples after them"* (20:29-30).

What an excruciating truth for Paul to have to face near the end of his days. I can't imagine how difficult that meeting was for such a loving shepherd, who had given his all for those believers. I cry, "Lord, this man has kept the faith. Let him go to Jerusalem and have a restful time with no burdens. Let him bask in the fellowship of the saints there. Let his final days be full of peace and quiet, free of pain and affliction."

Yet, within a week of arriving in Jerusalem, Paul was dragged out of the temple, putting the whole city in an uproar. Once again, the apostle was bound in chains. After all the trials and suffering he had endured, here came more ever-increasing demands on Paul's faith. It meant yet another imprisonment, another court appearance, another trial.

Because Paul appealed to the Emperor, he was now headed for Rome. But before that could happen, Paul faced even more suffering. The ship he was sailing on was wrecked by a mighty storm, with everyone aboard having to swim to shore. Eventually Paul made it to Rome, where he spent the next two years under house arrest, chained to a Roman soldier in a tiny, cheap, rented house. It was in such humble circumstances that Paul died a martyr.

Ever-increasing afflictions, demanding ever more steadfast faith, become a stumbling block to many believers.

Because of his sufferings, Paul was accused by fellow Christians of being chastened by God. They said his afflictions were the result of a lack of faith or because of some secret sin he was hiding. Moreover, the messenger of Satan appointed to harass Paul never let up, buffeting the apostle to his dying hour. As we watch Paul spending his last days in that tiny prison house – reaching the Jews who visited him, one by one, with the good news of Jesus – we find it impossible to explain why this beloved servant had to endure such extreme testing after years of suffering. Humanly, we can't comprehend it.

Personally, I think we simply can't explain why many righteous people face insurmountable sufferings. We'll never be able to state all the reasons why difficulties increase for those who love God deeply. We may think, "It's all meant to teach patience." Or, "It teaches God's people to trust him more." Yet, often when we say these things, they are nothing more than clichés. Certainly they are empty of meaning to those who are enduring critical crises.

I want to offer a special word to all who have come through floods and fiery furnaces of afflictions, and who are facing ever-increasing trials. I believe it is possible your time of testing may have nothing to do with chastening. Rather, it is this: *Something eternal – something having to do with your life in the new world to come – is at the center of your trial.* The battle you're enduring now is not about this world, not about the flesh, not about the devil. Rather, the warfare you're facing is preparation for your eternal service in glory. *You are being prepared for service on the other side.*

Think about it: The very day you committed your life to trust God, no matter the cost, he knew your present trial would come. He knew then – and he knows now – that you would love him through everything that comes at you. By grace you are determined to be an overcomer. And I'm convinced that right now everything you're facing points to the New Jerusalem. The apostle John writes of that time to come:

"There shall be no more curse: but the throne of God and of the Lamb shall be in it; and his servants shall serve him" (Revelation 22:3). *"There shall be no night there...and they shall reign for ever and ever"* (22:5). *"[He] hast made us unto our God kings and priests: and we shall reign on the earth"* (5:10). All of this speaks of activity. It suggests God is preparing us now for what he wants to entrust to us in the new world. Simply put, he has plans for us beyond our comprehension. Paul speaks of this when he says we will serve God continually, with all joy: *"He has raised us up together, and made us sit in heavenly places in Christ Jesus: that in the ages to come he might show the exceeding riches of his grace in his kindness towards us through Christ Jesus"* (Ephesians 2:6-7).

I believe our sufferings have the effect of weaning us from everything that is of this world.

The pains we are experiencing right now are awful birth pangs. God has allowed us to be so weakened of human strength that we may stop all striving and let him take us the rest of the way. There is an old gospel song: "By and by / When the morning comes / When all the saints of God are gathered home / We will tell the story how we've overcome / And we'll understand it better / By and by."

I have testified of God's goodness throughout my lifetime. And in the new world to come, I'm also going to tell my story all over heaven, of how real, near and merciful Jesus was to me in my worst times. That is the work we all have to look forward to in glory. Praise God!